Praise For Delores Mishleau's
Created To Nourish

Created to Nourish is a home run! At a time when the health of Americans is in steep decline, Delores Mishleau makes preparing fabulous food for the whole family fun and easy. Created to Nourish does more than introduce you to great nutrition. Comprehensive but not complicated, Created to Nourish will quickly become a trusted resource for a healthier and happier way of life.
John Bradshaw, President, It Is Written

This is the cookbook I've been looking for. My kids love the tasty recipes that are made with simple ingredients that I already have. Having cooked gluten free for years now, this cookbook adds many new recipes to my menu. I also love the suggested alternatives to some of the ingredients in each recipe. This really encourages me to experiment with each recipe. I would recommend this cookbook to anyone, whether they are gluten free or not.
Monica Larsen, gluten free cook and mother of four young children

I was delighted to explore Delores Mishleau's new gluten-free cookbook as I am gluten intolerant. It's a delicious collection of recipes that not only cater to those with gluten sensitivities but also bring a burst of flavor and creativity to the table.
The thoughtful combination of ingredients and easy-to-follow instructions make it accessible for both novice and experienced cooks.
This book is a must-have for anyone seeking to embrace a gluten-free lifestyle without compromising on taste or variety. Kudos to Delores Mishleau for crafting such a wonderful resource!
Edwin Nebblett MD, MPH, plant-based physician

Delores Mishleau's cooking is a true delight, and her new cookbook is no exception. For years, her delicious, nutritious, and health-conscious dishes have been a highlight at church potlucks and cooking seminars. What makes her work even more special is how she uses her culinary talents as a form of ministry, inviting people into her home for meals and cooking seminars that serve as both a warm introduction to the principles of Christian living and an opportunity to share the Word of God.
Her recipes are not only flavorful but also rooted in promoting well-being, making them perfect for anyone seeking to balance health and taste. Delores has a gift for bringing people together around the table, forming meaningful connections through the act of cooking and sharing meals. Her approach to food is holistic—nourishing both body and spirit.

I highly recommend her recipes and this cookbook to anyone, whether you're looking to improve your health, expand your culinary skills, or simply enjoy a wholesome, home-cooked meal. Delores's heart for ministry shines through in every recipe, making this book more than just a collection of dishes—it's a testament to her love for God and others.

Lena Toews, MA, PhD, Professor, Religion Division, Union Adventist University

Delores shares so much practical, godly knowledge about nutrition, diet, and healthful eating in her cooking classes, recipes, and ongoing whole-person interactions at home, church, or at the grocery store. The food is delicious and you know this is eating in ways that God will bless. Created to Nourish will be a joy to refer to time and time again to prepare tasty, healthy meals for one and all!

Tammy Adams, BSN, RN, Faith Community Nurse, Piedmont Park SDA Church

I praise God for my good friend Delores and this wonderful gift of a healthy cookbook that she has been inspired to create and share with the world. As the Bible so beautifully states, "Beloved, I wish above all things that thou mayest prosper and be in health" (3 John 1:2, KJV).

This cookbook contains recipes for healthy, plant-based meals that rely on easily sourced, everyday ingredients. These meals can be prepared quickly and efficiently, allowing them to fit into even the busiest lifestyles! In addition to cooking instructions, Delores has also shared creative ideas for recipe variations and even some helpful serving suggestions. I look forward to adding these recipes to my own table and sharing them with friends and family.

Thank you, Delores, for your wonderful gift to everyone seeking to implement and live a healthier lifestyle. May this cookbook be a blessing to all who receive it!

Donna McNeilus, plant-based home cook

CREATED TO Nourish

• Plant-Based Gluten-Free Recipes •

• Soy-Free Options •

Delores Mishleau

The author assumes full responsibility for the accuracy of all facts and quotations cited in this book. The opinions expressed in this book are the author's personal views and interpretations and do not necessarily reflect those of the publisher.

This book is provided with the understanding that neither the publisher nor the author is engaged in giving spiritual, legal, medical, nutritional, health, or other professional advice. If authoritative advice is needed, the reader should seek the counsel of a competent professional.

Copyright © 2025 Delores Mishleau
Copyright © 2025 TEACH Services, Inc.
Published in Calhoun, Georgia, USA
ISBN-13: 978-1-4796-1807-1 (Paperback)
ISBN-13: 978-1-4796-1892-7 (Hardback)
ISBN-13: 978-1-4796-1893-4 (Spiral)
ISBN-13: 978-1-4796-1808-1 (ePub)
Food Preparation: Delores Mishleau
Food Styling: Kathleen Chilson
Photography: Benjamin Mishleau
Photo Editor: Jonathan Mishleau
Author Photo on page # 7 (My Journeys page): Sharri Keller, Terra Sura Photography, TerraSura.com
Author Photo on back cover: Jonathan Mishleau, JEMPhotography

All scripture quotations are taken from King James Version. Public domain.

These recipes were created using U.S. measurements with metric measurements included for this publication. There should be no significant difference in the recipe outcome when using metric or imperial measures.

Contact the author at:
Email—DeloresMishleau@CreatedToNourish.com
Website—www.CreatedToNourish.com or https://1ref.us/ctn

Dedication

To my heavenly Father, who helped me complete this project! May He use this book to bless many cooks.

To my mother, Edna Rogers, who taught me the joy of cooking.

To my husband, Kent, who has been my "tester" for 33 years!

To my family: Curtis, Kelly, and Chesney; Kade, Courtney, Elgin, Edna, Helen, Irene, and Lydia; Luke, Savannah, Echo, and Bjorn; Jonathan; Benjamin and Myla; Elizabeth; Clarissa; and Silas. You are like rays of sunshine to my heart! May the food principles in this book guide and bless you with tasty food and good health!

To each of you who will be brave and creative in cooking these new recipes.

Contents

The Birth of
Created To Nourish

Plants were created to nourish us. To be well-nourished, we must eat daily, except for the occasional fast. The choices we make in the foods we eat will significantly impact the quality and quantity of the lives we lead. Created to Nourish delves into the divine master plan embedded in the composition and chemistry of the plants that provide strength for our daily tasks. There is a Divine Designer.

It all started at the beginning of this world. Around 6,000 years ago, my loving God designed and fashioned a world of beauty and diversity. He meticulously created plants with perfect combinations of carbohydrates, proteins, fats, vitamins, minerals, and phytochemicals to nourish all living creations. These plants were His gift to all life. He subsequently fashioned humans in His likeness to inhabit and enjoy what He had crafted. Humans were meant to be nourished by the plants of His creation. God designed our bodies to align with His plan, blessing us with the ability to think, reason, make choices, communicate, and prepare for eternity.

Our great Creator provided a blueprint—the Bible. As the world's first dietician, He designed the first meal plan for the first two people. In today's language, we would call it a plant-based diet. Each plant was designed with a unique combination of components needed to empower the newly-created beings. Additionally, God provided water (Gen. 1:2) and sunlight (Gen. 1:16) for optimal health. Recognizing our tendency to overwork, He created and sanctified a day of rest on the seventh day (Gen. 2:2). The first breath of life (Gen. 2:7) gave life to Adam, and our continued breathing sustains life today. Our bodies were designed to move and function more effectively when we exercise (Gen. 2:15). God encourages us to trust Him and to show that trust through obedience to His laws and principles (Gen. 2:17). With these few verses, God provided a comprehensive manual on how our bodies were designed to function.

God's perfect plan was marred by humanity's choice in Genesis 3. Adam and Eve opted for food that seemed right, looked right, and tasted right to them but was not in their blueprint. God intervened, presenting a plan for redemption—a theological plan for salvation. The rest of the Bible is a story of people and nations choosing to go against the divine blueprint and the sorrow and pain that came from this choice. Throughout the story, God continues to call people back to the blueprint and life He designed.

God is passionate about our physical, spiritual, and emotional health (3 John 1:2). As our Creator, He understands that compromised physical health affects spiritual and emotional well-being. God designed our bodies to heal and repair damages, utilizing plants to facilitate the process.

Food is both necessary and addictive, presenting a challenge that confronts us daily. The same enemy who disguised himself in the tree in the Garden of Eden still tempts us today, especially in the grocery store, luring us with smells, tastes, and old habits. Food has the power to make us sick and obese but also to fuel our bodies and minds for productive activities. For those looking to make a change, there is hope, there is help, and there is a Helper attuned to your thoughts about choosing better foods.

Habits define our actions without much thought. Picture a well-trodden animal path through a grassy area. If animals stop walking on the path, the grass will gradually grow back. You can form new habits, and old habits will fade with time. Prayer to the Creator can accelerate this process. You can establish new, healthier habits, and that's good news!

God, speaking through Paul, emphasizes in 1 Corinthians 3:16-17 that our bodies are God's temples. Paul also tells us that God wants to place the Holy Spirit in our minds because we've been purchased with a price—the death of Jesus to pay for our sins (1 Cor. 6:19–20). Our bodies are God's property. Making excellent food choices glorifies our Maker and often rewards us with good health, less disease, more energy, and increased joy. God created plants as a gift for us.

Created to Nourish has been written to encourage you to adopt a plant-based diet and accept the gift of plants from your Creator. It equips you with tools to make it a rewarding and feasible lifestyle. I also provide you with resources to connect with a community that is choosing plant-based foods and reaping the rewards. Welcome to an exciting adventure en route to a lifestyle nourished by God's gifts—plants!

Thank You

To my loving Creator:
Thank You for designing plants to nourish and heal our bodies. I am eternally grateful for the heritage You have given me of faith, family, and fantastic food passed down through the generations to me and now to others. Thank You for being my Saviour and for the promise of Your imminent return. I am thankful for the path You have led me on, introducing me to plant-based and gluten-free cooking and preparing me for this opportunity to share Your wisdom with others.

I want to express my gratitude for the practice run You provided when Pastor Michael, Betty J., and the congregation of the Piedmont Park Church invited me to conduct the Family Cooking Adventure back in January/February 2020. It is evident now that You have been shaping me for this book for many years. Thank You for Your patience as I continue my journey of honoring You by caring for my body. Amen.

To my dear husband, Kent:
Thank you for your unwavering patience and the countless hours you have sacrificed for me while I prepared food for photo shoots and worked endlessly on the computer. Your encouragement to share my passion for plant-based, gluten-free cooking with others means the world to me. It has been an honor to cook for you for 33 years. You are the best!

To my dearest Mother:
Thank you for patiently instilling in me the importance of the food we eat. Your countless hours of instruction, repeated until I fully grasped it, have shaped me into the plant-based cook I am today. I appreciate your encouragement and your countless prayers for me. Cooking for you brings me immense joy!

To Elizabeth, Clarissa, and Silas:
Your support around our home has given me the extra hours needed to complete this project. I cherish our time together in the kitchen, cooking, creating, and catching up. You are my food tasters and critics, and together, we are growing. I am proud of the progress each of you is making in your cooking skills, and I am thankful for the joy you bring into my life.

To Curtis, Courtney, Luke, Jonathan, and Benjamin:
You each have done more than you will ever know to mold me into the mom and cook I am today! Thank you for the opportunities you gave me in teaching you how to cook, for the countless hours of cooking together, and now for the privilege of coming to your homes and eating your delicious food. I am proud of each of you!

To Benjamin Mishleau:
Your positive attitude, the long hours getting just the right angle for each photo, and your never-ending encouragement are major reasons why there is a book today. You showed your faith in me by your actions. Thank you for believing in me more than I believed in myself. You make my heart sing for joy!

To Myla Mishleau:
Your dedication to this project has been unwavering and admirable. You worked diligently to make clean, concise, and easy-to-follow directions; you sought out amazing, gifted individuals like Brian Peoples, Ruth Campbell, Lisette Parks, and Kathie Chilson to assist you in this huge task. The countless hours spent collaborating with your husband, Benjamin; creating spreadsheets for organization; perfecting photo shots; unwavering positivity even as you finished dishes at 11 PM after a 6-hour photo shoot—all have played crucial roles in taking an idea all the way to the publisher. The title of this book is a testament to your creativity and vision. Thank you for your tireless dedication.

To Kathy Chilson:
This project allowed me to move past a casual friendship with you to a "sister of the heart." Driving long hours over hundreds of miles has resulted in a book with beautiful photos, most of which you arranged. How can I ever express to you how much your talents have meant to me and how they have made this book what it is? Thank you for making my food look picture-perfect! I appreciate your willingness to proofread the manuscript and the many helpful suggestions you offered. Most of all, thank you for all the prayers for me and this project.

To Lisette Parks:
You are my neighbor. You are my friend. You are my "sister of the heart." You were there for me from the beginning of this project, offering suggestions and guidance, praying for me, providing a treasury of dishes for Kathy to use in the pictures, and believing that what God had called me to do would be accomplished by His power. Your dishes helped add color and character to the photos. You have been a person of stability as I have navigated this project. Thank you for reading the manuscript and helping me fine-tune it! I am so thankful we are close by heart and distance!

To Jonathan Mishleau:
Behind the scenes and behind the computer screen, your attention to detail and great eye have added the finishing touches to the photos. I appreciate your help with this project.

To Leo and Ruth Campbell:
Thank you for using your many talents for God and for the success of this book. Your proofreading prowess, support, and prayers have been the "golden spike" that brought everything together for the completion of this book.

My Journey

I am a wife, happily married to a hard-working man who loves good food. As a mother to eight wonderful children, plus four married-into-the-family children, and blessed with eight grandchildren, my life revolves around the joy of cooking. I love to entertain our extended family and friends in our home and often contribute dishes to potlucks and parties. It is important to note that while I have a passion for healthy living through plant-based eating, I am not a doctor, nurse, or nutritionist. None of the statements in this book are intended to replace professional counsel.

My journey into the world of plant-based cooking began on the farm, where we always grew a sizable garden and tended to our own cows. Having grown up in a similar culture, my mother, the official family cook, instilled in me a love for delicious, wholesome food. Fresh produce from our garden, bathed in cream or baked with butter, made for delectable meals. We believed in the health of our cows and felt confident consuming our dairy products.

I well remember my dad saying that he believed there would soon be a time when there would be so much disease in animals that it would not be safe to use any dairy products. I always hated it when he said that. I loved how we cooked, and our food was delicious—ask any of our guests! It would be fair to say that I had a decidedly negative attitude toward people who did not enjoy dairy and eggs.

When I got married, my husband and I moved 1,000 miles away, where access to dairy products from cows we cared for was no longer available. I struggled with the taste of store-bought dairy, yet I lacked the know-how to cook without it. My mother visited us after the birth of our first son and introduced me to the soy milk featured in this book. From then on, I began making and using my soy milk instead of dairy milk. I found a farm to buy my eggs from until our fourth child was born, and Jennifer, who you will hear more about in this book, came to stay with our family. She taught me how to cook delicious food without eggs and dairy, and I fully embraced plant-based cooking. I again felt confident in my cooking and enjoyed eating my food!

For the next 23 years, I enjoyed cooking plant-based meals, sharing them at potlucks, and bringing home empty dishes. Occasionally hosting gluten-free friends, I made an effort to create enjoyable meals for them, never imagining that one day I also would be gluten-free.

About two years ago, I decided to try going gluten-free, initially thinking it would be a temporary experiment. I tried new recipes. I converted some of my favorite recipes. What you are reading is the result of many hours of cooking, critiquing by family and friends, and cooking more hours until all of us were happy with the delicious results. Potlucks and parties ended with compliments and empty dishes. Then the opportunity to share my experiences and tasty dishes opened up a new world for me. Created to Nourish was born! This book is a testament to the fact that miracles still happen, sometimes at the most unlikely time or in the most unlikely way!

Blessed with new inspiration and the courage to experiment in the kitchen, I slowly gained confidence in my gluten-free cooking. Then, my dear friend Emma Loberg called me with the idea of writing a cookbook. It is good I was down on my hands and knees, weeding in the garden, or I might have fallen over from the shock! Never in my life had I dreamt of writing a cookbook. Throughout the process of putting this book into your hands, I have been reminded that miracles still happen.

I believe that a diet centered on plant-based and gluten-free foods will benefit your well-being as significantly as it has mine. I challenge you to be brave, try these tested and loved recipes, and savor the joy of excellent and nourishing food!

Delores Mishleau

Ingredient Tips

Here are a few tips to keep in mind as you cook these recipes:

- **Agar Agar Powder:** This is an extract from seaweed. It is concentrated approximately four times as much as agar agar flakes. I use the powder in cooking these recipes, so please adjust the amounts if you are using flakes.

- **Bragg Liquid Aminos:** I use this ingredient in some recipes. If you use miso or another equivalent, you will need to adjust the recipes accordingly.

- **Butter:** I use Butterless Butter (p. 150) or Earth Balance.

- **Carob Powder/Carob Chips:** I use these ingredients instead of cocoa powder or chocolate chips. Carob is a nutritionally dense food, is not bitter, and does not contain caffeine or the chemical compounds found in cocoa.

- **Cornmeal:** Finding organic cornmeal with a fine, flour-like texture may be challenging. If I cannot find fine-textured cornmeal, I blend the coarser grind in my blender until it has the smooth texture I use in my recipes.

- **Ener-G Egg Replacer:** There are several egg replacers on the market. This is the one I use in these recipes. If you choose another egg replacer, the recipe results may be altered.

- **Gluten-free Flour Options:** When I began my gluten-free cooking adventure, I knew I would need to keep it simple, and I wanted my food to taste how I wanted it to taste. I bought a few flour mixes, thinking they would be the simplest. When everything I made with the flour tasted like garbanzo beans, I knew I would have to create my own flour blend. After some testing, I settled on the three main flours you will find in this book: almond flour (made from the whole nut minus the brown covering), sorghum flour, and tapioca flour. Feel free to try your own flour mixes, keeping in mind that different mixes may alter the recipe results. A few other flours that I have had luck with are:

  - **Hazelnut Flour:** Replacing one-fourth of the almond flour with this will add good flavor and will not significantly impact the recipe outcome.

  - **Millet Flour:** Replacing one-fourth to one-half of the almond flour with this will not change the recipe significantly and will provide the additional health benefits of millet.

  - **Arrowroot Flour:** Replacing half or the whole amount of tapioca flour with this will not significantly change the recipe outcome.

- **Flavorings:** I use alcohol-free flavorings in all of my recipes. Yes, they say that the alcohol evaporates in the cooking process; however, not all of the recipes in this book are cooked/baked. Alcohol-based flavorings also leave an aftertaste. For vanilla flavoring, powdered vanilla can be an economical alternative with no noticeable change to the flavor.

- **Lemon Juice:** For recipes that call for lemon juice, freshly squeezed is always best. If you are opting for bottled lemon juice, I encourage you to purchase one that does not contain lemon oil. There may be a frozen lemon juice option available where you shop. The frozen version likely will not have as many preservatives in it.

- **McKay's Vegan Chicken Style Seasoning:** I appreciate the savory flavor this seasoning delivers to my recipes. Feel free to use another type or make your own chicken-style seasoning. The flavor of the recipes will be somewhat altered.

- **McKay's Vegan Beef Style Seasoning:** I love the rich flavor this seasoning adds to my recipes. Feel free to use another type or make your own beef-style seasoning. The flavor of the recipes will be somewhat altered.

- **Nutritional Yeast:** This ingredient adds a "cheesy" flavor and extra-delicious nutrition. If you choose not to use nutritional yeast, you may find that some of the recipes work out well with an equal amount of ground hemp hearts. This will alter the taste somewhat.

- **Nuts and Seeds:** Unless otherwise indicated, the nuts and seeds I use are raw.

- **Oil:** All recipes are cooked with avocado oil unless otherwise noted.

- **Organic and Non-GMO:** I strongly recommend that you choose organic ingredients whenever possible. I highly recommend a non-GMO option if you cannot find an organic option.

- **Plant-Based Milk:** Although I use my own Homemade Soy Milk (p.23) recipe for all of the recipes in this book, the recipes will not be significantly altered if you choose to use a different plant-based milk in place of soy.

- **Salt:** I use Himalayan salt in all the recipes. If you choose to use a different salt, it may alter the flavor somewhat.

- **Tapioca or Cornstarch:** I use these two starches interchangeably in baking. When you need a thickener, I only recommend cornstarch, as it looks far more appetizing than tapioca when it cools.

Kitchen Tools

Each trade requires tools. The correct tools in your toolbox help you work efficiently and produce a great product. This "bare-bones" list will help you enjoy your time in the kitchen, be time-efficient, and create delicious food for your family.

- **Heavy-Bottomed Stainless Steel Cookware:** These kettles make it much easier not to burn the food you are cooking, particularly when you boil sauces and gravies. I do not recommend the use of aluminum cookware.

- **Stainless Steel Bakeware:** You likely will not find this at the cheapest store in town, but it will be worth the search and expense to have heavy-duty stainless steel cookie sheets, cake pans, etc. They will last a lifetime!

- **Powerful Blender:** In my years of cooking, I have worn out numerous blenders that could not handle the work I expected from them. Then my mother gave me a Vita-Mix. I was so excited! My blender is almost 10 years old now, and it has made cooking so much more enjoyable. I know the results will be excellent when I put ingredients in the jar to make smoothies, sauces, or waffles!

- **Stand Mixer:** When our second child was born, I was pleasantly surprised one day when my brother-in-law, Jack, arrived at the door, arms laden with boxes. To my amazement, he'd brought a KitchenAid mixer plus attachments! Knowing the extent of my cooking endeavors, Jack had thoughtfully chosen the perfect gift, which served me exceptionally well for over 20 years. Now I'm using my second, a gift from my husband.

- **A**dditionally, my mother gifted me a Bosch, which has been my go-to for heavy mixing projects, particularly bread, for over two decades. The KitchenAid and Bosch stand mixers are incredible investments. They are indispensable tools that contribute to your prowess as a cook and baker!

Features of This Book

Throughout this book, you will find:

- **Pertinent Bible Promises:** I personally chose each of these verses. Over the years, each has encouraged, strengthened, and comforted me as I have faced the deaths of family members, a miscarriage, financial challenges, and more. When life has been full of joy, these verses have been the "icing on the cake." God's Word is my daily food. I know it will bless you, too!

- **Recipe Variations:** Perhaps you are creative and like changing things up! You may also want or need to use different ingredients to meet the dietary needs of someone in your home. With each recipe, I have provided ideas for slight changes that can give you different flavors or set you on the path to creating your own fabulous recipe.

- **Planning Ahead:** I created this feature because I often need to plan meals several days or even weeks in advance. With this in mind, I wanted to give you ways to plan healthy meals ahead of time as needed.

- **Serving Suggestions:** Often, when I look at a recipe, I think, "That sounds delicious! What would I pair it with for a meal for my family? I need suggestions!" I trust you will find this helpful in using individual recipes to create tasty, filling, and nutritious meals.

- **Soy-Free Options:** More and more people are developing sensitivities to soy. While most of my recipes are or can easily be made soy-free, I have marked the few that require soy.

At the end of this book, you will find:

- **Learning More:** Here, you will find a small series I put together that includes Bible readings and spiritual insights that consider our diet and its impact on us. There are also resources from health professionals and researchers who can explain the science behind how plants were perfectly designed and created to nourish our bodies.

- **21-Day Meal Plan:** Want to cook healthy meals but don't know where to start? Here is a 21-day meal plan to help you begin your journey. Adjust the sides, use leftovers to save time, and create perfect meals for you, your family, and your friends.

Breakfast

MILLET BAKE

"O taste and see that the LORD is good: blessed is the man that trusteth in him." Psalms 34:8

I love this recipe because it's a nutritious breakfast I can prepare in the evening, set a timed bake on my oven, and wake up to a delicious, hot meal.

INGREDIENTS

1 c. (180 g) millet, uncooked

½ c. (80 g) dried apricots, chopped

½ c. (60 g) dried pineapple, chopped

½ c. (40 g) shredded coconut

2 c. (473 mL) + 3 c. (710 mL) water

⅔ c. (87 g) brazil nuts

1 tsp. (5 mL) vanilla

½ tsp. (3 g) salt

⅔ c. (170 g) dates

INSTRUCTIONS

1. In a covered casserole dish, stir to combine the first four ingredients.
2. Add the remaining ingredients with 2 c. (473 mL) of water to a blender and blend until very smooth and creamy. Pour over the millet mixture.
3. Pour the 3 c. (710 mL) of water over the mixture. Stir to combine.
4. Cover and bake for 1–1½ hours at 350°F (177°C) or until the millet is entirely soft in texture.

VARIATIONS

Customize this recipe to suit your family's preferences and ingredient availability. Experiment with various fruits and nuts to craft a unique and delightful dish!

SERVING SUGGESTIONS

This bake makes a great hot breakfast served plain or with Homemade Soy Milk (p. 23). Pair with Benjamin's Blueberry Muffins (p. 41), fresh fruit, and nuts. This dish can also be used as a light supper.

PLANNING AHEAD

Prepare this dish the night before and refrigerate overnight or set a timed bake on your oven so that you can have a hot breakfast ready the next morning. To reheat leftovers, cover with a lid and reheat it in the oven at 275°F (135°C) for 30 minutes.

GRANDMA'S BAKED RICE

"The LORD hath appeared of old unto me, saying, Yea, I have loved thee with an everlasting love: therefore with lovingkindness have I drawn thee." Jeremiah 31:3

My dear Grandma Rogers was such a great cook! Sometimes I would stay with her all by myself, and she would ask me what I wanted for supper. My standard answer was "rice." She made a dairy version of this recipe, and I loved it.

INGREDIENTS

4 c. (800 g) brown rice, cooked
(1⅓ c. (267 g) dry rice cooked
in 2¾ c. (651 mL) of water
+ ½ tsp. (3 g) salt)

1 c. (128 g) cashews

2 c. (473 mL) water

½ c. (80 g) raisins

½ c. (128 g) dates

¼ tsp. (1.5 g) salt

1 tsp. (5 mL) vanilla

2 tsp. (10 mL) maple flavoring

INSTRUCTIONS

1. In a covered casserole dish, stir to combine the rice and raisins.
2. Combine cashews, dates, water, and flavorings in a blender and blend until very smooth and creamy. Pour over the rice and raisins.
3. Bake, uncovered, for 1 hour at 350°F (177°C).

VARIATIONS

Swap cashews for almonds or brazil nuts. Try cooked millet instead of rice, skip the maple flavoring, or mix up dried fruits for varied colors and flavors.

SERVING SUGGESTIONS

Some of our family like to eat this with Soy Milk (p. 23). Others like to eat it just as it is. Team it up with Sunshine Muffins (p. 38), applesauce or home-canned peaches, and a handful of your favorite nuts or seeds for a delicious and nutritious breakfast or evening meal.

PLANNING AHEAD

You can prepare this dish a day in advance, refrigerate, and then bake as directed. It's also freezer-friendly and can be stored in an airtight container for up to a month. To reheat, thaw, cover with a lid, and place in the oven at 275°F (135°C) for 30 minutes.

SILAS' GRANOLA

"It is God that girdeth me with strength and maketh my way perfect." Psalms 18:32

Each of our children has mastered the art of making granola. Now, our youngest son, Silas, is learning the skill! He frequently asks if it's time to make it again, and my answer is often "Yes." It's so rewarding to teach my children skills for nourishing their bodies while incorporating math lessons.

◆

INGREDIENTS

6 c. (485 g) quick oats

1 c. (80 g) coconut, medium shred

1 c. (80 g) coconut, long shred

1 c. (140 g) sunflower seeds

1 c. (128 g) cashews

1 c. (112 g) almonds, sliced

1/2 c. (96 g) coconut sugar

2 tsp. (10 mL) vanilla

1/2 c. (120 mL) avocado oil

3/4 c. (255 g) honey

INSTRUCTIONS

1. Place all ingredients in a stand mixer with the beater attachment and combine on low speed.
2. Transfer granola to a large baking dish and bake at 350°F (177°C) for 10 minutes. Stir and continue baking in 5-minute intervals, stirring after each interval, until the granola is golden brown.
3. Remove from the oven and cool.

VARIATIONS

Experiment with different nuts in place of cashews. Substitute honey with maple syrup or agave. After baking, add a handful of chopped dried fruits like raisins or apricots for extra flavor.

SERVING SUGGESTIONS

Granola with Homemade Soy Milk (p 23) makes a quick and nutritious breakfast. Serve with Benjamin's Muffins (p. 41), fresh fruit, and raw nuts for breakfast to power through the morning. Need a quick, refreshing breakfast or dessert? Check out my recipe for Granola Parfaits (p 21).

PLANNING AHEAD

This granola can be stored in an airtight container for up to two weeks, so a large batch will last for one week or more.

GRANOLA PARFAITS

"Happy is he that hath the God of Jacob for his help, whose hope is in the LORD his God." Psalm 146:5

It's a joy to make these delicious parfaits with my children. They are fun, easy, and quick to assemble!

INGREDIENTS

6-8 parfait glasses

2 c. (218 g) Silas' Granola (p. 18)

1 recipe Coconut Whipped Cream (p. 190)

4 c. (175 g) fresh fruit; strawberries, raspberries, blueberries, peaches, etc.

INSTRUCTIONS

1. Create alternating layers by placing the ingredients in the glass by tablespoon. Start with granola, then whipped cream, fruit, and another layer of granola. Continue until the glass is filled. The top layer should be whipped cream with a garnish of granola and fruit
2. Chill until ready to serve.

VARIATIONS

Choose different whipped creams, such as my Tofu Whipped Cream (p.193), fruits, ingredients in the granola, nuts, ribbon coconut, etc. This is a great dessert/brunch to make with the children in your life!

SERVING SUGGESTIONS

This makes the perfect morning treat paired with some Tasty Tofu Scramble (p.30), and Potato Patties (p. 34). It also makes a lovely light dessert with any of the meals in this book.

PLANNING AHEAD

The whipped cream stores well in the refrigerator for a couple of days and the granola keeps well in an airtight container for several weeks. With these prepared ingredients available, you can whip up this recipe in just a few minutes.

INGREDIENTS

1/2 c. (86 g) soaked soybeans

2 c. (473 mL) boiling water

2 c. (473 mL) cold water

1/4 tsp. (1.5 g) salt

1/4-1/3 c. (60-80 mL) avocado oil

1-3 Tbsp. (21-63 g) honey (optional)

VARIATIONS

Add 1/2 teaspoon (2.5 mL) vanilla per quart of milk. Experiment with different sweeteners. For unsweetened milk, add only oil and salt to the milk base.

SERVING SUGGESTIONS

This milk is excellent for both cold and hot cereals. I use it in all my dishes that call for milk, and they turn out wonderfully!

PLANNING AHEAD

Unflavored milk will keep for at least seven days in the refrigerator, so you can make a batch weekly that will fulfill your family's milk needs for the week ahead.

INSTRUCTIONS*

1. Half fill the bottom pot of a double boiler with water and allow it to come to a boil over medium-high heat while you are completing step two.

2. Combine two cups of boiling water (from a separate saucepan or a teakettle) with the soaked soybeans in a blender and blend until smooth.

3. Place a cheesecloth over the top pot of the double boiler and pour the blended soybeans through the cloth into the pot. Some pulp will remain on top of the cheesecloth.

4. Pour 2 cups (473 mL) cold water through the pulp on the cheesecloth; this will collect in the top pot of the double boiler.

5. Squeeze any remaining liquid from the cheesecloth into the top pot of the double boiler, while keeping the pulp inside the cloth. The pulp may be discarded or saved for use in Saucy Soy Loaf (p. 70).

6. Cook the milk in the top pot of the double boiler for 15 minutes on medium heat. Do not boil.

7. If you will be using the milk within 3-4 days, partially fill a sink with cold water (adding ice, if possible). Place the pot of cooked milk in the cold water to chill quickly. Stir frequently. Once the milk has cooled, pour it into a blender.

8. Add salt, avocado oil, and honey (if you want sweetened milk) and blend on high for 2-3 minutes to combine.

9. Pour into a pitcher with a tight-sealing lid and store in the refrigerator. This flavored milk will keep for up to four days.

10. If you have made a larger batch than you will use within four days, pour the unflavored hot milk into canning jars immediately after cooking. Tightly screw on the lids. The jars will partially seal and can be kept in the refrigerator for 7-10 days. Blend with salt, oil, and honey, if desired, just before using.

*NOTES

1. To soak dry soybeans, cover with plenty of water so they will stay covered after they swell in size. Soak 12-24 hours, then drain. About 3 tablespoons of dry soybeans are adequate for a single recipe of soy milk. You may wish to soak a larger quantity of soybeans, then drain well and freeze in half-cup batches in freezer bags. The frozen soybeans can be used exactly like freshly soaked ones in this and other recipes.

2. If you wish to make a larger batch of milk than your double boiler will hold, use a large kettle as the bottom pot, and choose a metal bowl that fits into it to serve as the top pot.

HOMEMADE SOY MILK

"Call unto me, and I will answer thee, and shew thee great and mighty things, which thou knowest not." Jeremiah 33:3

Over 30 years ago, our first child was born, and my mother came to spend time with her first grandson. She had transitioned to a plant-based diet and was excited to share this soy milk recipe with me. Initially, I had reservations about dairy replacements, having grown up on a farm and thinking cow's milk was superior to anything else. Fortunately, I tried this recipe and liked it. The rest is history. For over 30 years, we've enjoyed milk for a quarter or less per quart. With a large family, that's a substantial savings. This recipe marked a turning point in my cooking and eating journey from vegetarian to wholly plant-based.

CREAMY FRUIT & RICE SALAD

"Wait on the LORD: be of good courage, and he shall strengthen thine heart: wait, I say, on the LORD." Psalm 27:14

I love serving this salad as a light supper because it is delicious and quick to put together, allowing me to enjoy conversation with family and friends. Rebeca, a dear friend from Peru, often joins us and shares her culinary treasures, like tamales. Rebeca inspires me with her sweet spirit and constant smile. Through our times shared in the kitchen and at the table with bowls of this salad, Rebeca has become a true "sister of the heart."

INGREDIENTS

3 c. (600 g) cooked brown rice

1 can (28 oz./793 g) peaches, drained and chopped

2 medium apples, cored and chopped

1 can (28 oz./794 g) pears, drained and chopped

2 oranges, peeled and chopped

3 c. (453 g) grapes, halved

1 can (20 oz./566 g) crushed pineapple, drained

1 recipe of Tofu Whipped Cream (p. 193)

INSTRUCTIONS

1. Mix the rice and fruit in a large serving bowl.
2. Add the whipped cream and mix to incorporate.

VARIATIONS

Choose firm fruits, but feel free to add other fruits, such as fresh blueberries, strawberries, etc. Avoid using soft fruits like bananas. To make it soy-free, use 1 recipe of Coconut Whipped Cream (p. 190) instead of the Tofu Whipped Cream (p. 193).

SERVING SUGGESTIONS

I like to serve this salad with various toppings. In small bowls, offer shredded coconut, sunflower seeds, carob chips, pumpkin seeds, dried cranberries, etc. It can be the centerpiece of your brunch with fresh raspberries or sliced strawberries on top. Planning a light supper with friends? This salad is sure to please.

PLANNING AHEAD

This salad is perfect to prepare several hours in advance and keep chilled, or you can make it and serve it immediately.

FRENCH TOAST

"Fear not, nor be dismayed, be strong and of good courage..." Joshua 10:25

French toast is a treat that's fun and quick to make with plant-based ingredients.

WET INGREDIENTS

2 1/2 c. (600 mL) Homemade Soy Milk (p. 23)

1/2 c. (64 g) cashews

2 Tbsp. (42 g) honey

2 tsp. (10 mL) vanilla

1/2 tsp. (3 g) salt

DRY INGREDIENTS

1/3 c. (47 g) sorghum flour

1/3 c. (37 g) almond flour

1/3 c. (40 g) tapioca flour

1/4 tsp. (0.6 g) xanthan gum

INSTRUCTIONS

1. Combine the wet ingredients in a blender and blend until smooth and creamy.
2. Add the dry ingredients and blend just long enough to incorporate.
3. Pour into a shallow container and dip a slice of your favorite gluten-free bread, completely covering both sides.
4. Fry both sides of each slice of bread on a non-stick griddle until golden brown.

VARIATIONS

Try using different nuts—Brazil nuts or almonds work well.

SERVING SUGGESTIONS

For a light meal, top with nut butter, fruit toppings such as Grandma Eunice's Blueberry Sauce (p. 181) or applesauce, and maple syrup. Serve with Quick Tofu Steaks (p. 33) and Potato Patties (p. 34) with American Ketchup (p. 173), along with fresh pineapple chunks, for a delicious brunch.

PLANNING AHEAD

This French toast is best eaten fresh but can be stored in an airtight container in the refrigerator for several days. Warm before serving.

HIGH-PROTEIN WAFFLES

As my children have grown up, they have each developed various physical fitness passions and goals. I have worked hard to find ways to add more protein into their diets, and these waffles have become a yummy staple for our breakfasts or light suppers.

◆

INGREDIENTS

2 1/4 c. (532 mL) water

1 c. (180 g) millet, uncooked

1 c. (172 g) soaked raw soybeans

1 Tbsp. (15 mL) avocado oil

1/2 tsp. (3 g) salt

2 Tbsp. (30 g) maple syrup

3 Tbsp. (21 g) golden flax

1/2 c. (40 g) quick oats

INSTRUCTIONS

1. Preheat your waffle iron.
2. Combine all ingredients in a blender and blend until creamy. Pour batter onto the waffle iron to form individual waffles.
3. Bake for 10-12 minutes or until golden.

VARIATIONS

Use quinoa instead of millet. Use honey or agave syrup instead of maple syrup. Add 1/4-1/2 cup (37-75 g) of your favorite nuts or seeds. To make the waffles soy-free, use 1 cup (112 g) almond flour instead of soybeans.

SERVING SUGGESTIONS

Top with maple syrup, Butterless Butter (p. 150), nut butter, Pineapple Date Jam (p. 182), Raspberry Jam (p. 185) (my favorite), Grandma Eunice's Blueberry Sauce (p. 181), applesauce, etc. Want to make brunch extra special? Dress up the waffles with various toppings—Tofu Whipped Cream (p. 193), toasted coconut, chopped pecans, finely chopped dried cranberries mixed with dried apricots, etc.

PLANNING AHEAD

Waffles freeze beautifully and can be conveniently warmed in the toaster, making them a perfect choice for a quick breakfast.

TASTY TOFU SCRAMBLE

"Now therefore go, and I will be with thy mouth,

and teach thee what thou shalt say." Exodus 4:12

Some of our children prefer savory over sweet breakfasts. Our daughter Clarissa particularly enjoys this recipe,

and now she is old enough to make it for the whole family!

◆

INGREDIENTS

2 Tbsp. (30 mL) avocado oil

1/2 c. (88 g) bell peppers, diced

1 lb. (454 g) firm tofu, drained and crumbled

1 Tbsp. (17 g) Bragg Liquid Aminos

1/2 c. (75 g) diced onion or 2 Tbsp. (12 g) onion powder

2 tsp. (2 g) McKay's Chicken Style Seasoning

1 Tbsp. (5 g) nutritional yeast flakes

1/8 tsp. (0.5 g) turmeric or (0.3 g) paprika

1 tsp. (3 g) garlic powder

INSTRUCTIONS

1. In a heavy-bottomed skillet, add 2 tablespoons (30 mL) oil.
2. Sauté the fresh veggies for 3–5 minutes on medium heat until they become soft.
3. Drain the water off the tofu, wrap the block in a paper towel, and gently squeeze to drain further. Crumble into the skillet with the veggies.
4. Add the seasonings and continue cooking for 8–10 minutes or until all water has evaporated.

VARIATIONS

Add your favorite veggies and seasonings to make this scramble your own. Some of my favorites are sliced black or green olives, diced tomatoes, and pimento pieces.

SERVING SUGGESTIONS

Pair with Potato Patties (p. 34), Toasty Oat Crackers (p. 49) topped with Butterless Butter (p. 150) and Pineapple Date Jam (p. 182), and fresh fruit for a great breakfast that will keep you satisfied for hours.

PLANNING AHEAD

Scrambled tofu is best enjoyed fresh, but leftovers can be refrigerated for several days. Warm before serving.

QUICK TOFU STEAKS

"If ye continue in my word, then are ye my disciples indeed; And ye shall know the truth, and the truth shall make you free." John 8:31-32

This is one of my favorite fast-food options. I enjoy cooking these with my children and frequently have one child do the dipping or coating while I do the other steps!

◆

INGREDIENTS

1 lb. (454 g) extra-firm tofu, drained

Bragg Liquid Aminos, in a shallow dish for first dipping

BREADING MIX

1/2 c. (56 g) almond flour

1/2 c. (70 g) sorghum flour

1/2 c. (64 g) cornstarch

1/2 c. (80 g) cornmeal

1 c. (80 g) nutritional yeast

2 Tbsp. (7 g) McKay's Beef Style Seasoning

2 Tbsp. (7 g) McKay's Chicken Style Seasoning

1 Tbsp. (4 g) Vegit

1 tsp. (2.4 g) onion powder

1/2 tsp. (1.5 g) garlic powder

INSTRUCTIONS

1. Slice the tofu block into 8 slices.
2. Dip the tofu slices in the Bragg Liquid Aminos for a few seconds.
3. Dip tofu slices in the breading mix, coating completely.
4. Fry the coated tofu on a lightly greased griddle until both sides are golden.
5. Alternatively, place the coated tofu on a lightly greased cookie sheet and bake at 350°F (177°C) for 20-30 minutes, depending on the level of crispiness desired.

VARIATIONS

Add 1/4-1/2 teaspoon (0.5-0.9 g) of your favorite herbs to the Bragg Liquid Aminos. Let the herbs soak for several hours before dipping the tofu. For a simpler flavor, coat the dipped slices in plain nutritional yeast before frying.

SERVING SUGGESTIONS

Use on sandwiches or homemade crackers as part of your brunch menu or as an entree.

PLANNING AHEAD

These are quick to make and taste best fresh. Prepare the breading mix ahead of time and store in a jar for ready use.

POTATO PATTIES

For whosoever shall call upon the name of the Lord shall be saved." Romans 10:13

These potato patties are a cherished part of our special family breakfasts—whether celebrating a family reunion, sharing a joyous occasion with friends, or for a holiday brunch!

◆

INGREDIENTS

4 lbs. (1.8 kg) shredded potatoes, fresh or frozen

1 Tbsp. (1.6 g) parsley flakes

1 medium onion, halved

1 c. (128 g) cashews

1/4 c. (4 g) McKay's Chicken Style Seasoning

1/2 tsp. (1.5 g) garlic powder

1 1/2 c. (355 mL) water

3 Tbsp. (36 g) potato flour

INSTRUCTIONS

1. Place potatoes and parsley in a large mixing bowl.
2. Combine the onion, cashews, seasonings, and water in a blender and blend until smooth.
3. Pour mixture over the potatoes, add the potato flour, and stir well to combine.
4. Shape into patties using a large ice cream scoop and flatten to 1/3-inch (0.85 cm) thickness.
5. Bake at 400°F (204°C) for 20–30 minutes, until the top is slightly crispy.
6. Flip and bake for 10–15 more minutes until golden brown.
7. Serve warm. Makes 24 patties.

VARIATIONS

Change the flavor profile by using fresh basil instead of parsley.

SERVING SUGGESTIONS

These patties are best served hot with American Ketchup (p. 173) or Plant-Based Mayonnaise (p. 174). Team them up with Tasty Tofu Scramble (p. 30), High-Protein Waffles (p. 29) with Grandma Eunice's Blueberry Sauce (p. 181), and Creamy Fruit and Rice Salad (p. 25) for a beautiful brunch that's sure to please.

PLANNING AHEAD

These potato patties are best enjoyed fresh, but if you have extras, wrap them individually in plastic wrap and freeze or refrigerate in a tightly sealed bag or container.

Muffins & Crackers

SUNSHINE MUFFINS

"I am come that they might have life, and that they might have it more abundantly." John 10:10

The combination of pineapple and coconut in these muffins makes me think of warm tropical islands and bright sunshine!

DRY INGREDIENTS

1 1/2 c. (120 g) shredded coconut

3/4 c. (102 g) pecan meal

1/2 c. (80 g) apricots, diced

1/2 c. (96 g) coconut sugar

1/2 c. (40 g) quick oats

1/2 c. (56 g) almond flour

1/2 c. (70 g) sorghum flour

1/2 c. (64 g) cornstarch

1 tsp. (2.5 g) xanthan gum

1 tsp. (6 g) salt

1 Tbsp. (12 g) baking powder

WET INGREDIENTS

1 1/2 tsp. (10 g) Ener-G Egg Replacer (mixed with 2 Tbsp. of hot water)

1 can (16 oz./454 g) crushed pineapple, drained

1 c. (240 mL) Homemade Soy Milk (p. 23)

1 tsp. (5 mL) vanilla

1/3 c. (75 g) Butterless Butter (p. 150), melted

INSTRUCTIONS

1. Place the dry ingredients in a stand mixer with a beater attachment and combine on low speed.
2. Add the wet ingredients to the dry mixture. Mix thoroughly.
3. Lightly grease muffin tins and fill cups halfway with batter.
4. Bake at 350°F (177°C) for 20-25 minutes or until muffin edges start to brown.
5. Allow muffins to cool for 10 minutes, then remove them from the muffin tins.

VARIATIONS

Replace half of the shredded coconut with coconut flour.

SERVING SUGGESTIONS

These muffins are delightful additions to breakfasts and brunches and can also be served as a dessert. Enjoy them with Pineapple Date Jam (p. 182) or almond butter.

PLANNING AHEAD

These muffins freeze well and can be stored in an airtight container for several weeks. To reheat, place them in a covered casserole dish or wrap each muffin in foil. Warm in a 300°F (149°C) oven for 15-20 minutes, and they'll taste almost as fresh as when first baked.

BENJAMIN'S BLUEBERRY MUFFINS

"Some trust in chariots, and some in horses: but we will remember the name of the LORD our God." Psalm 20:7

Benjamin has probably baked these muffins more than I have! He often made them as a lovely breakfast before church. His early talent in the kitchen led him on a path of cooking and baking regularly for groups large and small. Little did I know that teaching him the joy of cooking would lead him, at the age of 17, to bake at an event for over 3,000 people! Benjamin now enjoys crafting curries, including an Indian curry that has become a family favorite, and he loves to experiment with spices and herbs in all of his cooking.

◆

DRY INGREDIENTS

1 c. (81 g) quick oats

1/3 c. (47 g) sorghum flour

1/3 c. (37 g) almond flour

1/3 c. (40 g) tapioca flour

1/2 tsp. (1.3 g) xanthan gum

1 tsp. (6 g) salt

1/2 c. (96 g) coconut sugar

1 Tbsp. (12 g) baking powder

WET INGREDIENTS

1/3 c. (75 g) Butterless Butter (p. 150), melted

1 c. (240 mL) Homemade Soy Milk (p. 23)

1 tsp. (5 mL) vanilla

1 c. (188 g) blueberries, fresh or frozen

INSTRUCTIONS

1. Place the dry ingredients in a stand mixer with a beater attachment and combine on low speed.
2. Add the butter, milk, and vanilla. Mix thoroughly.
3. Incorporate blueberries, mixing just enough to distribute them evenly.
4. Bake in greased muffin pans at 350°F (177°C) for 20 minutes or until golden brown.

VARIATIONS

Replace the almond flour with hazelnut flour. Swap the butter substitute with applesauce. If using frozen blueberries, pat them dry and then dust with your choice of flour to keep the muffins from turning blue.

SERVING SUGGESTIONS

These make a great meal coupled with Creamy Fruit and Rice Salad (p.25) or Millet Bake (p. 14). Need something quick to go? Try some muffins, raw nuts, and fresh fruit for a nourishing and quick meal.

PLANNING AHEAD

These muffins freeze well, so consider making a double batch and storing some in the freezer for up to one month. To reheat, place them in a covered casserole dish or wrap each muffin in foil. Warm in a 300°F (149°C) oven for 15-20 minutes; they'll taste almost as fresh as when first baked.

MOM'S CORN BREAD

"Thou wilt keep him in perfect peace, whose mind is stayed on thee:
because he trusteth in thee." Isaiah 26:3

As a child, I cherished the special days when my wonderful mother baked a pan of corn bread. Over time, the corn bread transformed into muffins, but the delicious taste remained. My mother, a fantastic cook, crafts incredible meals from scratch using bountiful produce from the garden.

She continues to be my cooking hero!

◆

DRY INGREDIENTS

2 1/4 c. (360 g) cornmeal

1/2 c. (70 g) sorghum flour

1/2 c. (56 g) almond flour

1/2 c. (64 g) cornstarch

2 tsp. (5 g) xanthan gum

2 tsp. (12 g) salt

2 Tbsp. (24 g) baking powder

WET INGREDIENTS

12.3 oz. (349 g) firm silken tofu

1 c. (237 mL) water

1/2 c. (120 mL) avocado oil

1 c. (245 g) applesauce

1/4 c. (48 g) coconut sugar

INSTRUCTIONS

1. Combine the dry ingredients in a medium-sized bowl and stir well.
2. Place the wet ingredients in a blender and blend until smooth. Pour into the flour mixture and stir until thoroughly combined.
3. Spoon the batter into greased muffin tins to make 24 muffins or into a greased 9 x 13-inch (23 x 33-cm) pan or two 9 x 9-inch (23 x 23-cm) pans.
4. Bake at 350°F (177°C) for about 20 minutes, until golden around the edges.

VARIATIONS

Replace half of the almond flour with millet flour.

SERVING SUGGESTIONS

These muffins pair up well with Creamy German Potato Soup (p. 134), Mom's Navy Bean Soup (p. 138), Auntie Joan's Baked Beans (p. 86), or with a hearty salad such as Get-You-Started Kale Salad (p. 122) or Three-Bean Salad (p. 110) for a quick meal.

PLANNING AHEAD

These muffins are best enjoyed hot and fresh, but you can store leftover muffins in the freezer for up to one month. To reheat, place them in a covered casserole dish or wrap each muffin in foil.

BETTER BISCUITS

"Thou art a God ready to pardon, gracious and merciful, slow to anger, and of great kindness..." Nehemiah 9:17

Biscuits are a delightful and versatile bread, and I was pleased when I created this yummy version. I especially love eating these topped with my favorite gravy. Growing up on the Canadian prairies, I never ate biscuits and gravy. For breakfast? I thought gravy was reserved for mashed potatoes! My husband, Kent, who had lived in different parts of the USA, introduced me to the dish, and I have enjoyed it ever since.

INGREDIENTS

3/4 c. (84 g) almond flour

3/4 c. (105 g) sorghum flour

3/4 c. (90 g) tapioca flour

1 tsp. (2.5 g) xanthan gum

1 Tbsp. (12 g) baking powder

1 tsp. (6 g) salt

3 Tbsp. (42 g) Butterless Butter (p. 150)

1 c. (240 mL) Homemade Soy Milk (p. 23)

INSTRUCTIONS

1. Place the dry ingredients in a stand mixer with a beater attachment and combine on low speed.
2. Cut butter into bite-sized pieces and blend until it is evenly distributed in the flour.
3. Add milk and mix until well combined.
4. Use a serving spoon to form and drop biscuit dough onto a baking sheet.
5. Bake at 450°F (232°C) for 12–15 minutes until golden brown.

VARIATIONS

Substitute some of the almond flour with millet flour. For a nutty, whole-wheat flavor, consider adding 1–2 tablespoons (8.8–17.5 g) teff flour.

SERVING SUGGESTIONS

These biscuits taste incredible topped with Butterless Butter (p. 150) and your favorite jam. They will also go well with your favorite soup. Experience an American Southern breakfast by tearing them into pieces on your plate and topping them with Sue's Homestyle Gravy (p.161). Serve with Quick Tofu Steaks (p.33) and American Ketchup (p. 173).

PLANNING AHEAD

Double or triple the recipe and freeze any extra biscuits. They freeze well for up to one month. Thaw, then place in a covered casserole dish or wrap in foil. Warm in a 350°F (177°C) oven for 10-15 minutes.

DELICIOUS DATE CHEWS

"For I know the thoughts that I think toward you, saith the LORD, thoughts of peace, and not of evil, to give you an expected end." Jeremiah 29:11

I enjoy sharing these Delicious Date Chews with friends; they are always a hit! Friends like Tom and Alane, who for 10 years spoke at the annual family and marriage retreat we hosted with Restoration International, loved receiving a package of these treats for their journey home.

◆

DRY INGREDIENTS

1 1/3 c. (149 g) almond flour

1 1/3 c. (187 g) sorghum flour

1 1/3 c. (171 g) cornstarch

4 c. (324 g) quick oats

1/2 c. (96 g) coconut sugar

2 tsp. (12 g) salt

2 tsp. (5 g) xanthan gum

1 c. (80 g) shredded coconut

4 c. (1 kg) dates, chopped

WET INGREDIENTS

1 c. (240 mL) avocado oil

1 c. (237 mL) water

1 1/3 c. (149 g) walnuts

INSTRUCTIONS

1. Place the dry ingredients in a stand mixer with a beater attachment and combine on low speed.
2. Place the wet ingredients in a blender and blend until creamy (to have a little more crunch, blend for only 10–20 seconds).
3. Combine the blended mixture with the dry ingredients.
4. Adjust with water or flour for a stiff, non-sticky dough.
5. Roll out on a greased cookie sheet to 1/4-inch (0.64-cm) thickness.
6. Cut or use cookie cutters to form desired shapes.
7. Bake at 350°F (177°C) for 15 minutes; remove crackers that have turned golden on the edges and then bake remaining crackers for 10 more minutes.
8. Continue until all crackers are golden brown.
9. Cool on a wire rack.

VARIATIONS

Have fun experimenting with different kinds of flour. Replace walnuts with Brazil nuts.

SERVING SUGGESTIONS

Enjoy these crackers on their own or with almond butter and Pineapple Date Jam (p. 182). Packed with nutrients, they make a perfect on-the-go meal with raw nuts and fresh fruit, or pair them with Grandma's Baked Rice (p. 17), raw nuts, and applesauce.

PLANNING AHEAD

These crackers last 5–10 days in a tightly closed container. They may be refrigerated or frozen to extend their freshness. To refresh, place frozen crackers on a cookie sheet and bake at 350°F (177°C) for 5 minutes.

TOASTY OAT CRACKERS

"Is any thing too hard for the LORD?..." Genesis 18:14

Fiber-packed oats, complemented by the healthy fats of walnuts and sesame seeds and topped off with a hint of sweetness, will leave you reaching for just one more.

◆

INGREDIENTS

3 c. (243 g) quick oats

1/2 c. (56 g) almond flour

1/2 c. (70 g) sorghum flour

2 tsp. (5 g) xanthan gum

1 tsp. (6 g) salt

1/2 c. (64 g) cornstarch

1/3 c. (37 g) walnuts, ground

2 Tbsp. (40 g) light molasses

1/3 c. (80 mL) avocado oil

1/2 c. (118 mL) warm water, or more as needed

1/4 c. (48 g) sesame seeds, hulled, for garnish

INSTRUCTIONS

1. Place the oats, flours, gum, and salt in a stand mixer with a beater attachment and combine on low speed.
2. Place the remaining ingredients in a blender and blend.
3. Combine both sets of ingredients in the stand mixer, adding water if needed to mix well. It should form a dough ball that cleans the sides of the bowl and is not sticky.
4. Divide into 2 balls and roll out on greased cookie sheets.
5. Lightly roll the sesame seeds onto the crackers. You may cut the crackers into the desired size before baking. You may also use cookie cutters to lightly imprint the crackers. Children love marking the crackers with fun cookie cutters.
6. Bake at 325°F (177°C). Begin checking the crackers after 15 minutes.
7. Remove golden crackers, and return cookie sheet to the oven. Continue baking until all of the crackers are done.

VARIATIONS

Substitute 1/4 cup (28 g) almond flour with millet flour. Use pecans or Brazil nuts instead of walnuts. Opt for maple syrup instead of molasses for a lighter-colored cracker.

SERVING SUGGESTIONS

These crackers are incredibly versatile and pair well with savory and sweet toppings. Because of their ability to complement a variety of meals, you might be tempted to make a large batch.

PLANNING AHEAD

These crackers will store in an airtight container in a cool place for up to one month or can be frozen. To refresh, place frozen crackers on a cookie sheet and bake at 350°F (177°C) for 5 minutes.

SUNFLOWER CRACKERS

"He shall feed his flock like a shepherd: he shall gather the lambs with his arm, and carry them in his bosom, and shall gently lead those that are with young." Isaiah 40:11

When I was a child, my mom made a German deep-fried treat called "Roll Kuchen" with flour, cream, eggs, and salt when we had watermelon. With a plant-based twist, these sunflower crackers bring back those childhood memories, creating a perfect combo with sweet, cold watermelon for a summer supper!

INGREDIENTS

1 1/3 c. (149 g) almond flour

1 1/3 c. (187 g) sorghum flour

2 tsp. (5 g) xanthan gum

3/4 tsp. (5 g) salt

1 c. (140 g) sunflower seeds, partially ground (at least half of the seeds should be ground as fine as flour; the rest should be partially ground to add a tasty crunch to your crackers)

1 1/3 c. (171 g) cornstarch

1/2 c. (120 mL) avocado oil

3/4 c. (177 mL) cold water or more

INSTRUCTIONS

1. Place the first six ingredients in a stand mixer with a beater attachment and combine on low speed. Add oil and mix well.
2. Slowly add water until the dough forms a ball and does not stick to the edges.
3. Divide into two balls, roll out on a greased cookie sheet. You may cut the crackers into the desired size before baking. You may also use cookie cutters to lightly imprint the crackers. Children love marking the crackers with fun cookie cutters.
4. Bake at 330°F (166°C). Check after 15 minutes; remove golden crackers on the edges. Return cookie sheet to the oven to continue baking until all the crackers are done. When baked completely, the crackers will have a light golden color and will be completely released from the cookie sheet.

VARIATIONS

Add 1 tablespoon (8.8 g) teff flour for more whole wheat flavor. Sprinkle coarse salt over the crackers to add texture and taste.

SERVING SUGGESTIONS

These crackers pair well with both sweet and savory toppings. They are an excellent complement to Judy's Cheese (p. 154) and a bowl of your favorite soup.

PLANNING AHEAD

Plan to make a large batch of these crackers. They store well in an airtight container in a cool place for up to one month or can be frozen. To refresh, place frozen crackers on a cookie sheet and bake at 350°F (177°C) for 5 minutes.

COURTNEY'S CRACKERS

"Thy mercy, O LORD, is in the heavens; and thy faithfulness reacheth unto the clouds." Psalm 36:5

These delicate crackers, crafted by our daughter Courtney, reflect the joy we've shared in cooking over the years. Now, she's passing on the culinary tradition to her five children, showcasing skills from artisan bread to intricate wedding cakes. Watching her pass this knowledge on to her children is one of my great joys.

INGREDIENTS

2/3 c. (75 g) almond flour

2/3 c. (93 g) sorghum flour

2/3 c. (85 g) cornstarch

1/2 tsp. (1.3 g) xanthan gum

1/2 tsp. (3 g) salt

1/3 c. (73 g) refined coconut oil

1/2-2/3 c. (118-158 mL) cold water

INSTRUCTIONS

1. Place ingredients in a stand mixer with a beater attachment and thoroughly combine.
2. Roll out the dough on a lightly greased cookie sheet.
3. Cut into squares or use cookie cutters to create decorative shapes.
4. Bake at 350°F (177°C), checking the crackers after 10 minutes.
5. Remove the outer crackers as they brown and continue baking the remaining crackers until done.

VARIATIONS

Replace 1 tablespoon (8.8 g) of one of the flours with teff flour for whole wheat flavor. Substitute cornstarch with arrowroot starch. Sprinkle rolled-out crackers with coarse salt and your preferred herbs, like Italian seasoning. Gently press salt and seasoning into the dough with a rolling pin.

SERVING SUGGESTIONS

These crackers are versatile and can be enjoyed with Judy's Cheese (p. 154), a bowl of hot soup, or with Creamy Fruit and Rice Salad (p. 25) for a light meal.

PLANNING AHEAD

Handle these crisp crackers gently. They freeze well in an airtight container for up to one month. To refresh, place frozen crackers on a cookie sheet and bake at 350°F (177°C) for 5 minutes.

Entrees & Proteins

CLARE'S CLASSIC ENCHILADAS

"Be not afraid, neither be thou dismayed: for the LORD thy God is with thee whithersoever thou goest." Joshua 1:9

Our daughter Clarissa (Clare) enjoys helping me make this recipe, which she thinks is the best food I ever make! Clare loves to create smoothies and bake savory dishes. It is a joy for me as a mom to teach my children how to prepare nourishing food for their bodies.

FILLING

4 c. (800 g) cooked brown rice

6 c. (1 kg) cooked pinto beans

1 lb. (454 g) firm tofu, drained and crumbled

2+ Tbsp. (12+ g) chili powder*(depending on the spice level desired)*

2 1/2 tsp. (2 g) dried basil, ground

2 large onions, chopped and sautéed in 2 Tbsp. (30 mL) avocado oil until soft

CHEESE SAUCE

1/3 of a 16-oz. (454 g) package firm tofu, drained

1/2 c. (64 g) cashews

1/2 tsp. (1.5 g) garlic powder

1 tsp. (2.4 g) onion powder

1/4 c. (32 g) cornstarch

2 Tbsp. (10 g) nutritional yeast flakes

1 c. (237 mL) water

1 1/2 c. (363 g) salted canned tomatoes, whole or diced

1 tsp. (6 g) salt

1 medium poblano pepper, seeded (last batch only)

TOPPING

1 can (16 oz./454 g) enchilada sauce

1/2-1 c. (90-180 g) black olives, sliced

INSTRUCTIONS

1. Place the cheese sauce ingredients in a blender and blend. Make the recipe three times, adding the poblano pepper to the last batch. As each recipe is finished, pour into a large bowl or beaker.
2. In a large mixing bowl, stir the filling ingredients and 1 batch (or 1/3) of the cheese sauce until well combined.
3. Spread 1 1/4 cups (240 mL) cheese sauce on the bottom of an 11 x 15-inch (27 x 38-cm) baking dish.
4. Heat your griddle to 375°F (191°C) and warm each tortilla for 20 seconds on each side to soften.
5. Place a serving spoon of filling in the middle of a tortilla. Fold the left and right edges over the filling, then place seam side down in the prepared pan.
6. Repeat for each tortilla, nestling them together until there is a single layer packed into the pan.
7. Pour the remaining cheese over the top of the enchiladas.
8. Use a spatula between each enchilada to ensure the cheese is in between and completely covering each enchilada.
9. Pour the enchilada sauce over the top of the enchiladas. Mix the cheese and sauce with a spatula to create color swirls.
10. Add olive slices, pressing them partially into the cheese to keep them from burning in the oven.
11. Bake, uncovered, at 350°F (177°C) for 1 hour.

VARIATIONS

Use different beans in the filling. Experiment with various hot peppers to achieve the exact level of heat and taste that makes your family smile at the first bite!

SERVING SUGGESTIONS

Enchiladas pair well with Mexican Rice (p. 58), cooked green beans, and Aunt Greta's Green Salad (p. 109) for a festive meal. Get the family together or invite some friends over to share this large dish.

PLANNING AHEAD

You can freeze the fully prepared pan by covering it with plastic wrap and placing it in an airtight bag. Thaw before baking and then bake as directed.

MEXICAN RICE

"Beloved, I wish above all things that thou mayest prosper and be in health, even as thy soul prospereth." 3 John 1:2

This recipe has the perfect amount of flavor and spice for someone who grew up eating potatoes on the Canadian prairies!

◆

INGREDIENTS

3 medium onions, diced

1 green bell pepper, seeded and diced

1/2 c. poblano pepper, seeded and finely chopped

4 Tbsp. (60 mL) avocado oil

2 cans (28 oz./794 g each) petite diced tomatoes

1 small can (4 oz /113 g) green chili peppers

4 c. (764 g) white uncooked rice

2 Tbsp. (36 g) salt

4 c. (946 mL) water

INSTRUCTIONS

1. In a large heavy-bottomed pot, sauté the onions, poblano pepper, and bell pepper in the oil.
2. Add remaining ingredients to the pot and bring to a boil, stirring constantly.
3. Transfer to a lidded casserole or covered baking dish.
4. Bake at 350°F (177°C) for 30–45 minutes until the rice is soft and fluffy.

VARIATIONS

Experiment with different varieties or amounts of peppers to find the perfect spice flavor and level for your family. Try quick brown rice instead of white rice for extra nutrition.

SERVING SUGGESTIONS

Mexican Rice pairs well with Clare's Classic Enchiladas (p.,56), cooked green beans, and Aunt Greta's Green Salad (p. 109) for a "South of the Border" meal! Try pairing it with Get-You-Started Kale Salad (p. 122) and Mom's Corn Bread (p.42) for another delicious meal option.

PLANNING AHEAD

You can freeze this dish after baking. Store it in an airtight bag and thaw before warming it in a covered casserole dish for 30 minutes at 350°F (177°C).

CREAMY ALFREDO

"In my Father's house are many mansions: if it were not so, I would have told you.
I go to prepare a place for you." John 14:2

This delicious pasta dish is a family favorite. When I serve it to guests, I often hear that it is "better than the dairy version," and I agree!

◆

INGREDIENTS

1 lb. (0.5 kg) gluten-free pasta

1 c. (128 g) cashews

1 c. (237 mL) + 1 1/2 c. (355 mL) water

2 Tbsp. (16 g) cornstarch

2 Tbsp. (7 g) McKay's Chicken Style Seasoning

1/2 tsp. (1.2 g) onion powder

1 tsp. (6 g) salt

1/2 tsp. (0.4 g) dried basil

INSTRUCTIONS

1. Cook pasta in salted, boiling water until al dente. Drain pasta, pour into a large bowl, and set aside.
2. Bring 1 cup (237 mL) water to boil in a heavy-bottomed saucepan.
3. Place the sauce ingredients in a blender and blend until smooth and creamy.
4. Pour the blended mixture into the boiling water, stirring constantly with a whisk until it comes to a boil.
5. Remove from heat and pour over the drained pasta.
6. If desired, transfer to a 9 x 13-inch (23 x 33-cm) pan and bake at 350°F (177°C) for 30-60 minutes, depending on how crispy you want the dish to be.

VARIATIONS

Experiment with different gluten-free pasta options. If opting for almonds instead of cashews, include an extra 2 tablespoons (30 mL) avocado oil.

SERVING SUGGESTIONS

This pairs well with Quick Burgers (p. 82), cooked carrots, and Get-You-Started Kale Salad (p. 122). For an Italian dinner, pair this recipe with steamed broccoli and Garlic Butter (p. 153) toast.

PLANNING AHEAD

This Alfredo is delicious the second time around when baked. Place leftovers in a covered dish and bake at 350°F (177°C) until the edges turn golden.

MAC & CHEESE BAKE

"Like as a father pitieth his children, so the LORD pitieth them that fear Him. For he knoweth our frame; he remembereth that we are dust." Psalm 103:13–14

My mom introduced me to this plant-based mac and cheese recipe when I was about 5 years old. It quickly became a family favorite and has now become a favorite with my own family.

INGREDIENTS

1 lb. (0.5 kg) gluten-free pasta

SAUCE

1 c. (237 mL) water

1 c. (128 g) cashews

1 1/2 tsp. (9 g) salt

1 1/2 tsp. (3.6 g) onion powder

1/4 c. (60 mL) avocado oil

3 Tbsp. (36 g) sesame seeds

1/4 c. (20 g) nutritional yeast flakes

1/4 c. (60 mL) lemon juice

2 c. (484 g) canned tomatoes, whole or diced

INSTRUCTIONS

1. Cook pasta in salted boiling water until al dente. Drain pasta, pour into a large bowl, and set aside.
2. Place sauce ingredients in a blender and blend for 3 minutes until smooth and creamy.
3. Mix drained pasta with sauce and pour into a prepared 9 x 13-inch (23 x 33-cm) pan.
4. Bake, uncovered, at 350°F (177°C) for 1 hour or until golden.

VARIATIONS

Experiment with different gluten-free pasta varieties; brown rice pasta is my preferred choice for this recipe. Arrange the dry pasta in the baking dish, add 1 cup (237 mL) water, pour the sauce over the pasta, and follow the baking instructions above. If opting for almonds instead of cashews, include an extra 2 tablespoons (30 mL) avocado oil.

SERVING SUGGESTIONS

This mac and cheese pairs well with Auntie Joan's Baked Beans (p. 86) and Colorful Cucumber Salad (p. 121).

PLANNING AHEAD

This dish can be frozen before baking, and it's delightful both hot and cold, depending on the pasta type used.

JONATHAN'S MANICOTTI

"The LORD upholdeth all that fall, and raiseth up all those that be bowed down." Psalm 145:14

Years ago, during a busy period of building a new home, caring for newborn Jonathan, and running a home business, we were blessed to have a teenager named Jennifer join our lives. Jennifer introduced me to delicious plant-based cooking, inspiring my transition to fully plant-based. This recipe, a gift from Jennifer, is a cherished part of those memories. This is our son Jonathan's favorite entree, and I often have the joy of making it for him when he visits. Jonathan is the "king" of making amazing salads, which are the perfect side to this manicotti!

INGREDIENTS

14 gluten-free manicotti noodles, uncooked

4 c. (900 g) Elizabeth's Pasta Sauce (p.170)

FILLING

2 lbs. (907 g) firm tofu, drained

2 Tbsp. (11 g) Italian seasoning

1/2 Tbsp. (1 g) basil, ground

2 tsp. (6 g) garlic powder

1 tsp. (2.4 g) onion powder

2 Tbsp. (30 mL) avocado oil

1 1/2 tsp. (9 g) salt

2 Tbsp. (10 g) nutritional yeast flakes

1 Tbsp. (3.5 g) McKay's Chicken Style Seasoning

1 large onion, diced and sautéed in a small amount of oil

INSTRUCTIONS

1. Pour 1 1/2 cups (372 g) pasta sauce into the bottom of 9 x 13-inch (23 x 33-cm) baking dish.
2. Place the filling ingredients in a stand mixer with a beater attachment and mix on medium speed for 4–5 minutes.
3. Transfer part of the mixture to a large pastry bag and cut off one corner.
4. Fill the manicotti by squeezing the bagged mixture into both ends of each noodle.
5. Arrange the stuffed noodles in the prepared pan and cover with the remaining sauce.
6. Use a spatula to spread the sauce between and over the noodles so that each noodle is completely covered with sauce.
7. Pour 1 1/2 cups (355 mL) water over the noodles for added moisture.
8. Bake at 350°F (177°C) for 1 hour, covering with foil only if it appears to be drying too quickly on the surface.

VARIATIONS

Use different types of gluten-free fillable pasta to create other variations of this classic manicotti.

SERVING SUGGESTIONS

Manicotti makes a beautiful entree when eaten with Garlic Butter (p. 153) toast or rolls, cooked sweet peas or green beans, and Aunt Greta's Green Salad (p. 109).

PLANNING AHEAD

Prepare this dish a day or two in advance or freeze it for up to one month. To cook when frozen, thaw and then follow the steps for baking.

TOFU MEATBALLS

"Call upon me in the day of trouble: I will deliver thee, and thou shalt glorify me." Psalm 50:15

Over the years, this recipe has been a favorite to make and serve. Spaghetti is a fun recipe for people of all ages, and these meatballs add flavor and protein for a nutritious and satisfying meal.

◆

INGREDIENTS

2 Tbsp. (30 mL) avocado oil

1 small onion, diced

1 lb. (454 g) firm tofu, drained and crumbled

1 c. (81 g) quick oats

2 Tbsp. (32 g) almond butter

3 Tbsp. (50 g) Bragg Liquid Aminos

1/4 c. (15 g) fresh parsley, minced, or 1 Tbsp. (2 g) parsley flakes

1 Tbsp. (3.5 g) McKay's Chicken Style Seasoning

1 tsp. (2 g) ground cumin

INSTRUCTIONS

1. Sauté the onion in oil until soft.
2. Place the onion and remaining ingredients in a stand mixer with a beater attachment and combine.
3. Add more oats if the mixture is too soft.
4. Let the mixture sit for 5 minutes.
5. Prepare a cookie sheet with a silicone baking sheet or a light coating of plant-based oil spray.
6. Use a small cookie scoop to form balls and drop dough onto the prepared cookie sheet.
7. Bake at 350°F (177°C) for 45 minutes or until the edges turn golden.

VARIATIONS

Omit the cumin for a more neutral flavor. Try cashew butter instead of almond butter.

SERVING SUGGESTIONS

These Tofu Meatballs are a great way to add protein to your spaghetti dish. Cook your favorite gluten-free spaghetti and top with Elizabeth's Pasta Sauce (p. 170) and a few meatballs. Bake toast with Garlic Butter (p. 153), cook some green beans, and mix up Shredded Cabbage Salad (p. 114) or Aunt Greta's Green Salad (p. 109) for a hearty meal.

PLANNING AHEAD

These meatballs freeze well before baking. Drop them on a cookie sheet, freeze, and then store in a tightly sealed bag. When you need them, place them frozen on a greased cookie sheet and bake for 50-60 minutes.

CASHEW NUT LOAF

"Commit thy way unto the LORD; trust also in him; and he shall bring it to pass." Psalm 37:5

I remember my mom making this loaf when I was a child. Now I often make it for my own children and grandchildren, who enjoy it as much as I do!

INGREDIENTS

1 large onion, diced

4 Tbsp. (60 mL) avocado oil

1 c. (128 g) cashews, rinsed

2 c. (480 mL) Homemade Soy Milk (p. 23), unsweetened

2 Tbsp. (17 g) Bragg Liquid Aminos

1 tsp. (6 g) salt

1/2 tsp. (0.7 g) dried sage

1 tsp. (2 g) celery seed

2 c. (400 g) cooked brown rice

4 slices gluten-free bread

INSTRUCTIONS

1. In a small skillet, sauté diced onions in avocado oil until soft.
2. Combine cashews, milk, and seasonings in a blender and blend until creamy.
3. Dice four slices of bread into small squares.
4. In a large mixing bowl, combine blended ingredients, sautéed onions, rice, and bread cubes, mixing well with a large spoon.
5. Transfer the mixture to a greased 9 x 13-inch (22 x 33-cm) baking dish and bake, uncovered, at 350°F (177°C) for 1 hour.

VARIATIONS

Change the flavor by using walnuts instead of cashews, increasing the sage to 1 teaspoon (1.4 g), and omitting the celery seed.

SERVING SUGGESTIONS

This loaf pairs well with baked Irish or sweet potatoes, served with salt and Butterless Butter (p. 150). Add some Shredded Cabbage Salad (p. 114) and cooked sweet peas for a delicious meal.

PLANNING AHEAD

This loaf freezes well, making it convenient for quick meals. Prepare a double batch and freeze it either baked or unbaked. Store in a tightly sealed bag for 1–2 months. If baked, cut into portion-sized pieces before freezing for easy thawing and reheating.

SAUCY SOY LOAF

"But God commendeth his love toward us, in that, while we were yet sinners, Christ died for us." Romans 5:8

This loaf is one I have made countless times for potluck events. It is rewarding to bring home an empty dish and a list of recipe requests!

◆

INGREDIENTS

2 1/2 c. (430 g) soaked raw soybeans (may be frozen)

1 1/2 c. (355 mL) water

1 c. (136 g) walnuts or pecan meal

1 tsp. (6 g) salt

1 Tbsp. (3.5 g) McKay's Beef Style Seasoning

1/4 c. (66 g) Bragg Liquid Aminos

2 medium onions, diced

8 celery stalks, sliced

2 Tbsp. (30 mL) avocado oil

2 c. (162 g) quick oats

SAUCE

1 can (12 oz./340 g) tomato paste

2 c. (473 mL) water

1 tsp. (6 g) salt

1 tsp. (1 g) oregano

1/2 tsp. (1.5 g) garlic powder or to taste

INSTRUCTIONS

1. Place the soybeans, water, and seasonings in a blender and blend until smooth. Set aside.
2. Sauté onions and celery in the avocado oil.
3. Pour the soybean blend into a medium-sized mixing bowl and add the veggies, meal, and oats. Stir well to combine.
4. Pour into a greased 11 x 15-inch (27.94 x 38.1-cm) baking dish.
5. Add the sauce ingredients to the blender and blend until smooth. Spread over the loaf.
6. Bake, uncovered, at 350°F (177°C) for 1 hour.

VARIATIONS

Replace the soaked soybeans with soybean pulp left over from making Soy Milk (p. 23).

Replace some or all of the nut meal with ground hemp hearts.

SERVING SUGGESTIONS

This loaf is an excellent entree for a wholesome dinner. Choose a salad, such as Crunchy Carrot Salad (p. 117), to bring a splash of color to your plate. Roast a batch of Grandma Marge's Potatoes (p. 101) and serve with a side of cooked vegetables like corn, steamed green beans, or broccoli.

PLANNING AHEAD

This loaf freezes well either before or after baking. Keep thawing time in mind when cooking or reheating from frozen.

LISETTE'S LENTIL LOAF

Cast thy burden upon the LORD, and he shall sustain thee: he shall never suffer the righteous to be moved."

Psalm 55:22

This recipe is the creation of my dear friend Lisette P. She blesses my life in as many ways

as there are lentils in this loaf.

◆

LENTILS

1 lb. (0.5 kg) dry lentils

2-3 bay leaves

1/8 tsp. (0.3 g) cumin

1/2 tsp. (0.7 g) dried sage

1/2 tsp. (1.5 g) turmeric

1/8 tsp. (0.3 g) smoked paprika

1 tsp. (6 g) salt

LOAF

1/4 c. (60 mL) avocado or olive oil

1 medium onion, diced

1 1/2 c. (390 g) cooked lentils

1 c. (240 mL) Homemade Soy Milk
(p. 23), unsweetened

1/2 c. (68 g) pecan meal

3 large garlic cloves, minced

1 1/2 c. (42 g) corn flakes

1/2 tsp. (3 g) salt

1 tsp. (0.7 g) dried sage

INSTRUCTIONS

1. Sort and rinse 1 pound (0.5 kg) lentils. Soak for a few hours or overnight.
2. In a large heavy-bottomed pot, add 4 cups (946 mL) water and the soaked lentils with lentil seasonings.
3. Cook for 30 minutes, until lentils are soft and all extra water is absorbed.
4. Sauté onion in oil until tender.
5. Place 1 1/2 cups (390 g) cooked lentils in a large mixing bowl with the sautéed onions and oil. Add the remaining loaf ingredients and stir to combine.
6. Transfer to a lightly greased 9 x 9-inch (23 x 23-cm) baking dish. Bake, uncovered, at 350°F (177°C) for 35-45 minutes or until golden.

VARIATIONS

Replace pecan meal with walnut meal. Adjust the amounts and types of herbs in both the lentils and the loaf. You may use 1/2 cup (40 g) onion flakes instead of raw onion. The recipe may be doubled to fill a 9 x 13-inch (23 x 33-cm) baking dish.

SERVING SUGGESTIONS

This loaf is the cornerstone of a great meal. Add some of your favorite in-season veggies and a salad for a meal that is sure to please.

PLANNING AHEAD

Half-bake the loaf at 330°F (166°C) for 20-25 minutes to allow it to set. Afterward, cool and either freeze or refrigerate. Before eating, reheat and finish baking at 250°F (121°C) for up to 1 hour. Set the baking dish on a baking sheet to prevent the bottom from burning during reheating.

SUNNY POTATO LOAF

"For thou art my hope, O Lord GOD: thou art my trust from my youth." Psalm 71:5

I can still see my mom standing in her kitchen, using a green plastic grater to grate the potatoes for this loaf.
Soon, our family of four would be seated around the table with garden-fresh produce and Sunny Potato Loaf.
We would say grace and eat before returning to our many jobs on the farm.

INGREDIENTS

1 c. (240 mL) Homemade Soy Milk (p. 23), unsweetened

1 medium onion, diced

1 c. (140 g) sunflower seeds

1 c. (112 g) walnuts

1 1/2 tsp. (9 g) salt

1 c. (140 g) raw potato, grated

2 c. (180 g) gluten-free bread, cubed

INSTRUCTIONS

1. Place the first five ingredients in a blender and blend until smooth.
2. Pour into a large mixing bowl with the potato and bread and stir thoroughly to combine.
3. Pour into a greased 9 x 9-inch (23 x 23-cm) baking dish and bake, uncovered, at 350°F (177°C) for 1 hour.

VARIATIONS

Use only sunflower seeds if you have a nut allergy. Experiment with different kinds of bread or cracker crumbs.

SERVING SUGGESTIONS

Creamy Dilly Potatoes (p. 97) or Stuffed Sweet Potatoes (p. 102) team up nicely with this loaf, as do mashed potatoes with Sue's Homestyle Gravy (p. 161). Serve with Crunchy Carrot Salad (p. 117) or Colorful Cucumber Salad (p. 121). Add some fresh or frozen corn to round out the meal.

PLANNING AHEAD

This loaf freezes well after baking. Make a double batch, cut into serving-size portions for your household, and freeze. Thaw and warm before serving.

QUICK NUT ROAST

"For the Lord GOD will help me; therefore shall I not be confounded: therefore have I set my face like a flint, and I know that I shall not be ashamed." Isaiah 50:7

The clock is ticking...it will soon be time for a hearty meal for the family. This loaf delivers!

◆

INGREDIENTS

3 Tbsp. (45 mL) avocado oil

2 medium onions, diced

2 1/2 c. (250 g) celery, thinly sliced

3/4 c. (102 g) walnuts or pecans

1 1/2 tsp. (9 g) salt

1/2 tsp. (0.7 g) dried sage

3 c. (720 mL) Homemade Soy Milk (p. 23), unsweetened

1 1/4 tsp. (0.9 g) dried basil

3/4 c. (105 g) sunflower seeds, ground

3 c. (270 g) gluten-free bread, cubed

INSTRUCTIONS

1. Sauté onions and celery in oil until soft.
2. Place nuts, salt, sage, milk, and basil in a blender and blend to combine.
3. In a large bowl, stir to combine the blended ingredients with sautéed veggies, sunflower seeds, and bread.
4. Pour the mixture into a greased 9 x 13-inch (23 x 33-cm) baking dish.
5. Bake, uncovered, at 350°F (177°C) for 1 hour.

VARIATIONS

Nut allergy? Use hemp hearts instead of nut meal. Try gluten-free cracker crumbs as part of the 3 cups (270 g) bread cubes. You may use 3 cups (726 g) canned tomatoes (whole or diced) instead of the milk.

SERVING SUGGESTIONS

Create a wholesome meal by including sides of baked Irish or sweet potatoes, cooked carrot circles, and Aunt Greta's Green Salad (p. 109).

PLANNING AHEAD

This roast can be frozen before or after baking. Consider cutting it into serving-sized portions after it is baked and before freezing. Remove from the freezer when needed. It will stay fresh for 1-2 months in the freezer.

HOLIDAY TOFU ROAST

"Fear not: for, behold, I bring you good tidings of great joy, which shall be to all people." Luke 2:10

As my cooking journey evolved to being plant-based, I wondered what I would cook for Thanksgiving and other holidays. I trust your family will have as much joy gathering together to eat this tasty loaf as our family has. Food traditions and family memories go hand in hand!

◆

INGREDIENTS

3 Tbsp. (45 mL) avocado oil

6-8 celery stalks, sliced

1 large onion, diced

2 lbs. (907 g) firm tofu, drained

3/4-1 c. (173-230 g) Plant-Based Mayonnaise (p. 174)

1/4 c. (66 g) Bragg Liquid Aminos

3/4 tsp. (5 g) salt

1/2 tsp. (1.5 g) garlic powder

2 tsp. (3 g) dried sage

4 c. (360 g) gluten-free bread, cubed

INSTRUCTIONS

1. Sauté onions and celery with oil in a medium-sized skillet until soft.
2. Crumble tofu into a large mixing bowl and add remaining ingredients. Stir to combine.
3. Pour the mixture into a greased 9 x 13-inch (23 x 33-cm) baking dish.
4. Bake, uncovered, at 350°F (177°C) for 1 hour.

VARIATIONS

Add a can of diced black olives to the loaf mixture before baking. For a lovely garnish, slice some olives and gently press them into the roast after it is in the pan.

SERVING SUGGESTIONS

Create the ultimate holiday spread by adding sides of mashed potatoes with Sue's Homestyle Gravy (p. 161), cooked green beans, Cranberry Relish (p. 178), and Aunt Greta's Green Salad (p. 109).

PLANNING AHEAD

This roast freezes well both before and after baking. To jump-start a future meal, consider cutting it into serving-sized portions after baking. Freeze them and then remove from the freezer when needed.

CURTIS' OAT BURGERS

"I am the light of the world: he that followeth me shall not walk in darkness, but shall have the light of life." John 8:12

Our oldest son, Curtis, has made these so often that I am sure he memorized the recipe! And each meal he made for our family has been a blessing! Now he loves to cook for his own family and friends and enjoys hosting special celebrations several times a year.

◆

INGREDIENTS

1 medium onion, diced

2 Tbsp. (30 mL) avocado oil

1 2/3 c. (400 mL) Homemade Soy Milk (p. 23), unsweetened

2 Tbsp. (10 g) nutritional yeast flakes

1 c. (112 g) walnuts

1 1/2 Tbsp. (25 g) Bragg Liquid Aminos

1 1/2 tsp. (9 g) salt

1/2 tsp. (1.5 g) garlic powder

1/2 tsp. (0.7 g) dried sage

2 c. (162 g) quick oats

1/4 c. (120 g) hemp hearts

INSTRUCTIONS

1. Sauté the onion in oil until soft.
2. Place the milk, nuts, and seasonings in a blender and blend to combine. Pour into a medium-sized bowl. Add oats and hemp hearts. Allow the mixture to rest for 5 minutes.
3. Drop spoonfuls onto a lightly greased cookie sheet, forming 2-2 1/2-inch (5-6.4-cm) burgers.
4. Bake, uncovered, at 350°F (177°C) for 30 minutes. Flip with a spatula and bake for an additional 10 minutes.
5. Alternatively, you can fry the burgers on a lightly greased griddle until golden brown on both sides, about 8-10 minutes per side.

VARIATIONS

Try substituting half of the walnuts with sunflower seeds. Or omit the garlic powder and include 2 cloves freshly squeezed garlic sautéed with the onion.

SERVING SUGGESTIONS

These burgers are so versatile! They're delicious on a gluten-free bun with all the fixings, along with Oven French Fries (p. 98) or a baked potato, fresh or frozen corn, and Beet Salad (p. 113) or Colorful Cucumber Salad (p.121).

PLANNING AHEAD

You can make a double batch of these burgers, baking enough for a meal, and refrigerate the remaining batter so you can bake up a fresh batch of burgers for the next meal. Baked burgers can be frozen in an airtight container for 4-6 weeks. For the best flavor and texture, thaw and reheat in a covered casserole dish or covered with foil at 350°F (177°C) for 15 minutes before serving.

QUICK BURGERS

"Thou hast also given me the shield of thy salvation: and thy right hand hath holden me up, and thy gentleness hath made me great." Psalm 18:35

These burgers are a frequent go-to recipe for our family. Overflowing with herbs and nuts, they are a tasty fill-me-up kind of burger.

◆

INGREDIENTS

1 large onion, diced

2 Tbsp. (30 mL) avocado oil

4 1/2 c. (1 L) boiling water

1 1/2 c. (168 g) walnuts or pecans, ground or finely chopped

1 1/2 c. (210 g) sunflower seeds, ground

1 tsp. (0.7 g) dried basil

4 1/2 c. (360 g) quick oats

1/2 tsp. (0.5 g) dried oregano

1/2 c. (40 g) nutritional yeast flakes

1/2 c. (66 g) Bragg Liquid Aminos

1 1/2 tsp. (3 g) Italian seasoning

INSTRUCTIONS

1. In a small saucepan, sauté the onion with a bit of oil.
2. Bring water to a boil in a medium saucepan.
3. Add all ingredients, including the onion, to the boiling water. Mix well and remove from heat.
4. Allow to cool for 5-10 minutes.
5. Form into burgers about 1/3 inch (0.85 cm) thick on a greased cookie sheet.
6. Bake, uncovered, at 350°F (177°C) for about 30 minutes or until well done.
7. Flip the burgers with a spatula and bake for an additional 10 minutes.
8. Alternatively, fry patties on a lightly greased griddle for 8-10 minutes on each side.

VARIATIONS

Create a nut-free burger by exchanging nuts for hemp hearts.

SERVING SUGGESTIONS

Serve these burgers on your favorite gluten-free bun with all the sandwich fixings—Plant-Based Mayonnaise (p. 174), American Ketchup (p.173), and veggies, paired with Oven French Fries (p. 98). These burgers are also excellent served with baked potatoes, Zucchini Discs (p. 94), and Beet Salad (p. 113).

PLANNING AHEAD

These burgers are best enjoyed fresh from the oven. The recipe makes a generous batch, allowing you to bake what you need for a meal. Refrigerate the remaining batter for 3–4 days and bake it when needed. Alternatively, you can freeze the baked burgers in an airtight container for 4–6 weeks. For the best flavor and texture, thaw and reheat in a covered casserole dish or covered with foil at 350°F (177°C) for 15 minutes before serving.

SUNNY BURGERS

"I, even I, am he that blotteth out thy transgressions for mine own sake, and will not remember thy sins." Isaiah 43:25

This is an excellent dish to make ahead and bring to potluck events. Bring the burgers in a casserole dish and your broth in a jar. Pour the broth over the burgers and bake as usual.

◆

BURGERS

2 1/2 c. (202 g) quick oats

1 c. (140 g) sunflower seeds, ground

1 Tbsp. (5.9 g) onion powder

2 Tbsp. (30 g) psyllium husk powder

1 1/4 c. (296 mL) hot water

BROTH

4 c. (946 mL) water

1/3 c. (89 g) Bragg Liquid Aminos

2 Tbsp. (3.2 g) parsley flakes

1 Tbsp. (3.5 g) McKay's Chicken Style Seasoning

INSTRUCTIONS

1. Combine burger ingredients in a mixing bowl and let sit for 5 minutes to allow the oats to absorb the water.
2. Use wet hands to shape the mixture into burgers.
3. Brown both sides evenly on a hot, lightly greased griddle.
4. Place the fried burgers in a baking dish that can be covered.
5. Combine broth ingredients in a small saucepan and bring to a boil. Pour over the burgers.
6. Cover the dish and bake at 350°F (177°C) for 1 hour.

VARIATIONS

Replace some of the sunflower seeds with hemp hearts or some of your favorite nuts.

SERVING SUGGESTIONS

These burgers pair nicely with Oven French Fries (p.98), cooked green beans, and Crunchy Carrot Salad (p. 117). They are best eaten hot.

PLANNING AHEAD

These burgers freeze well after they are fried. Place them in an airtight bag and store in the freezer for up to one month. Taking them out of the freezer and warming them by putting them into boiling broth will jump-start your meal prep.

AUNTIE JOAN'S BAKED BEANS

"The LORD is my strength and my shield; my heart trusted in Him, and I am helped: therefore my heart greatly rejoiceth; and with my song I will praise Him." Psalm 28:7

As a child, I cherished the gatherings with my dad's family. I have wonderful memories of birthdays, Mother's Days, holidays, and simple family gatherings. The menu often included Auntie Joan's Baked Beans, Aunt Greta's Green Salad, and my mother's Creamy Potato Salad—a feast fit for a king!

INGREDIENTS

2 c. (320 g) dry navy beans, cooked in salted water until soft.

¼ c. (80 g) light molasses
(I like Grandma's Molasses)

¼ c. (48 g) coconut sugar

1¾ c. (414 mL) bean water
(liquid from cooking the beans)

1 medium onion, diced

1 clove garlic, minced

1 - 28-32 oz. (794-908 g) can diced tomatoes, salted

INSTRUCTIONS

1. Combine all of the ingredients in a bean pot or other ceramic or glass-covered casserole dish.
2. Bake at 250°F (121°C) for 5-7 hours.

VARIATIONS

Try different kinds of beans such as pinto or lima. Use maple syrup instead of molasses.

SERVING SUGGESTIONS

Auntie Joan's Baked Beans evoke memories of summer, picnics, and cherished moments with loved ones. Pair them with Creamy Potato Salad (p. 125), Beet Salad (p. 113), and Kathy's Confetti Salad (p. 118) for a delightful picnic. If it's raining or too cold for a picnic, enjoy them with Thanksgiving Sweet Potatoes (p. 105), cooked green beans, and Shredded Cabbage Salad (p. 114).

PLANNING AHEAD

These baked beans store well in the refrigerator for several days, so they can be made in advance and ease the busyness of your day. They are tasty hot or cold!

LUKE'S LENTILS

"But they that wait upon the LORD shall renew their strength; they shall mount up with wings as eagles; they shall run, and not be weary; and they shall walk, and not faint." Isaiah 40:31

As a homeschool mom, I discovered that quick and nourishing meals were essential. This recipe became a staple that my children, especially Luke, learned early in their cooking adventures. Now a skilled cook, he spent many enjoyable hours in the kitchen with me, and I'm grateful for those moments.

INGREDIENTS

2 1/2 c. (591 mL) water

3/4 tsp. (5 g) salt

1/2 c. (95 g) uncooked lentils

1 medium onion, diced

1/2 c. (96 g) white rice or quick-cooking brown rice

2 Tbsp. (30 mL) avocado oil

INSTRUCTIONS

1. Combine water, salt, and lentils in a 2-quart (2 L) saucepan. Cover and bring to a boil, then reduce heat to maintain a simmer.
2. In a separate pan, sauté the onion, rice, and oil. Once the onion is tender and the rice begins to brown, add to the lentils.
3. Continue cooking, covered and with minimal stirring, for about 20 minutes, until water is absorbed and both the rice and lentils are fully cooked. Adjust the heat as necessary to prevent scorching.

VARIATIONS

Add 1–2 cloves of freshly-crushed garlic to the onion and rice while they are sautéing.

SERVING SUGGESTIONS

Our family loves this dish hot or cold. When it is hot, it pairs well with Grandma Marge's Potatoes (p. 101), Glazed Beets (p. 93), and Aunt Greta's Green Salad (p. 109). Some members of our family like to top it with Elizabeth's Pasta Sauce (p. 170).

PLANNING AHEAD

Make a double batch and warm up the leftovers for a day or two.

Veggies
&
Side Dishes

GLAZED BEETS

"I am the LORD thy God which teacheth thee to profit, which leadeth thee by the way that thou shouldest go."
Isaiah 48:17

Beets were among my dad's favorite vegetables. He relished the glazed beets that my mom made. Dad appreciated uncomplicated meals, hard work, and engaging in conversations to discover people's stories. While he could have pursued a prominent career as a journalist or interviewer, he remained devoted to raising his children in the countryside, instilling godly values through shared work and worship. I am eternally thankful for my parents' sacrifices, prioritizing a lifestyle centered on knowing God and serving others over financial gains.

INGREDIENTS

3-4 medium beets, cooked, peeled, and diced into 1/4-inch (0.6 cm) squares

1 c. (237 mL) water

2 Tbsp. (30 mL) lemon juice

2 Tbsp. (42 g) honey

1/2 tsp. (3 g) salt

THICKENER

1/2 c. (118 mL) water

2 Tbsp. (16 g) cornstarch

INSTRUCTIONS

1. Heat the beets and water together in a heavy-bottomed saucepan. When they come to a boil, add the remaining ingredients.
2. Whisk the water and cornstarch in a cup and pour over the cooking beets, stirring constantly until they come to a boil.
3. Boil for an additional minute before removing from heat.

VARIATIONS

Use agave instead of honey.

SERVING SUGGESTIONS

These beets taste so amazing that you will want to pair them with numerous potato dishes, entrees, and salads. I recommend them as a side to any of the entrees in this book.

PLANNING AHEAD

This dish is best eaten when hot and freshly made.

ZUCCHINI DISCS

"But Jesus beheld them, and said unto them, With men this is impossible; but with God all things are possible."
Matthew 19:26

This is one of my favorite ways to fix zucchini! It is also a great recipe to make with your children. Many children love getting their fingers wet and sticky, and this recipe gives the perfect opportunity for both!

INGREDIENTS

2 medium zucchini

1/2 c. (120 mL) avocado oil

1/2 c. (120 mL) Homemade Soy Milk (p.23), unsweetened

1/4 c. (28 g) almond flour

1/2 c. (70 g) sorghum flour

1/4 c. (32 g) cornstarch

1 Tbsp. (4 g) McKay's Beef Style Seasoning

1 Tbsp. (4 g) McKay's Chicken Style Seasoning

1 tsp. (3 g) onion powder

1/4 tsp. (1 g) garlic powder

INSTRUCTIONS

1. Slice the zucchini into 1/4-inch (0.64-cm) discs.
2. Blend oil and milk in a blender for 1 minute. Pour into a bowl and set aside.
3. In a gallon-sized bag, mix the remaining ingredients.
4. Dip the zucchini discs in the oil mixture. Allow excess to drip off the zucchini, then place in the breading bag and shake to coat.
5. Place discs on a preheated cookie sheet and bake for 15–20 minutes at 400°F (204°C). Flip the discs and bake an additional 5–10 minutes or until the discs achieve the desired crispiness and golden-brown color.

VARIATIONS

Replace 1/4 cup (28 g) almond flour with millet flour. Add 1 teaspoon (2 g) Italian seasoning to the dry ingredients.

SERVING SUGGESTIONS

These discs make a great side with many types of entrees. I like them with pasta, potatoes, and as a side to a hearty soup. You will likely find that they disappear quickly!

PLANNING AHEAD

These discs are best when hot and fresh and do not freeze well.

CREAMY DILLY POTATOES

"Withhold not thou thy tender mercies from me, O LORD: let thy lovingkindness and thy truth continually preserve me." Psalm 40:11

These potatoes speak of summer to me! As a child, I remember going to the field with my mother and brother, Gordon. These delicious potatoes were often part of our packed lunch. We would ride along on a little bench seat in the tractor cab while my mother cultivated the fields. Those were the days when farmers cultivated more and sprayed less—the "good old days"!

◆

POTATOES

4–5 lbs. (1.8–2.3 kg) red potatoes

1 medium onion, diced

1 small handful of fresh dill, cut into 1-inch (2.5-cm) pieces OR 1 Tbsp. (5.6 g) dried dill weed

1 1/2 tsp. (9 g) salt

CASHEW SAUCE

2 c. (473 mL) water

1/2 c. (64 g) cashews

1 tsp. (6 g) salt

2 tsp. (5 g) onion powder

INSTRUCTIONS

1. Scrub and cut potatoes into 1-inch (2.5 cm) cubes. Fill a 6-quart (6 L) heavy-bottomed pot halfway with potato cubes.
2. Chop the onion into medium-sized pieces and add it with the fresh or dried dill to the potatoes.
3. Pour enough water over the potatoes to have 1–1 1/2 inches (2.5–3.8 cm) at the bottom of the kettle.
4. Sprinkle salt over the potatoes and simmer until soft, about 30–40 minutes. Stir occasionally to ensure they do not stick or scorch.
5. While the potatoes are cooking, place the sauce ingredients in a blender and blend until smooth and creamy.
6. Add the sauce to the potatoes and cook just long enough to bring to a boil.
7. Remove from heat and serve.

VARIATIONS

I like to use garden-fresh potatoes for this dish, along with fresh dill. Another delicious option is to use a small handful of fresh parsley instead of the dill and add three medium-sized carrots cut into 1/4-inch (0.6-cm) thick circles.

SERVING SUGGESTIONS

These potatoes are delicious with Curtis's Oat Burgers (p. 81), Colorful Cucumber Salad (p. 121), and fresh corn on the cob for a true taste-of-summer meal.

PLANNING AHEAD

Dilly Potatoes are best served fresh, but leftovers are still yummy.

OVEN FRENCH FRIES

"Be not afraid nor dismayed by reason of this great multitude; for the battle is not yours, but God's."

2 Chronicles 20:15

These simple fries are delicious for an occasional summertime treat!

◆

INGREDIENTS

5 large red potatoes

1/4-1/3 c. (53-71 g) olive oil

1 tsp. (6 g) salt

2 tsp. (5 g) onion powder

INSTRUCTIONS

1. Cut the potatoes into 1/4-inch (0.6 cm) square fries.
2. Place all ingredients in a large mixing bowl and toss to coat the potatoes with oil and seasonings.
3. Spread the fries in a single layer on a baking tray.
4. Bake at 400°F (204°C) for 35 minutes, then flip with a spatula. Continue baking for an additional 20-30 minutes until fries reach the desired level of crispiness.
5. Serve promptly.

VARIATIONS

Minced garlic can be added to the potato mixture before baking. Try adding 2-3 tablespoons (5.2-7.8 g) taco seasoning along with the salt, mixing thoroughly with the potatoes before baking.

SERVING SUGGESTIONS

These fries taste great served with American Ketchup (p. 173). Make them a side to Quick Burgers (p. 82) with all the trimmings and Shredded Cabbage Salad (p. 114) for a classic American lunch.

PLANNING AHEAD

These fries are best made and served promptly. They do not freeze well.

GRANDMA MARGE'S POTATOES

"My sheep hear my voice, and I know them, and they follow me." John 10:27

Grandma Marge is one special "adopted" grandma! Her name evokes many pleasant memories of singing the good old hymns together, enjoying birthday parties, chatting about gardening, and more. Grandma Marge's Potatoes are iconic at the potlucks of the little church in Minnesota we used to attend. Whenever our family talks about our friends there, someone quickly mentions these potatoes, and everyone agrees they are the best! Perhaps it's the seasonings, but I think it's all the love put into each pan of her potatoes. Sometimes we're a bit jealous of Grandpa Dale, who gets to feast on these roasted potatoes regularly.

INGREDIENTS

8 c. (1.1 kg) potatoes, cubed

6 large garlic cloves, minced

3 Tbsp. (40 mL) olive oil

3 Tbsp. (44 mL) water

3 Tbsp. (10 g) fresh rosemary, loosely chopped, or 1 Tbsp. (6 g) dried rosemary

1 tsp. (6 g) salt

INSTRUCTIONS

1. Place the cubed potatoes in a large bowl. Mix the remaining ingredients together and pour over the potatoes. Toss to coat.
2. Bake in a Dutch oven or 9 x 13-inch (23 x 33-cm) covered baking dish at 400°F (204°C) for about 1 hour. The potatoes should have a nice golden-brown color.

VARIATIONS

Experiment with different kinds of potatoes (red, russet, Yukon gold, or purple) to find the potato you enjoy most with this recipe. Mix several types of potatoes together, leaving their peels on, for a colorful pan of roasted potatoes. Add 6 whole garlic cloves to roast with the potatoes.

SERVING SUGGESTIONS

These delicious roasted potatoes pair nicely with Lisette's Lentil Loaf (p. 73), Quick Tofu Steaks (p. 33), or Luke's Lentils (p. 89). Add some steamed broccoli topped with Pimento Cheese Sauce (p.157) and Beet Salad (p. 113) for a colorful and tasty meal.

PLANNING AHEAD

You can prepare the potatoes, cover them with cold water in a sealed container, and place them in the refrigerator for up to one day before draining and adding the seasoning mixture.

STUFFED SWEET POTATOES

"Ask, and it shall be given you; seek, and ye shall find; knock, and it shall be opened unto you." Luke 11:9

There can never be too many ways to enjoy the wonderful flavor and nutrition of sweet potatoes!

INGREDIENTS

4 large sweet potatoes

2 tbsp. (28 g) Butterless Butter (p.150)

2 tbsp. (24 g) coconut sugar

¼ tsp. (0.7 g) ground cinnamon

⅓ c. (53 g) raisins

⅓ c. (36 g) toasted pecans, chopped
To toast pecans: Bake at 350°F (177°C) for 5-8 minutes in a shallow baking pan. Stir once.

INSTRUCTIONS

1. Bake the potatoes on a foil-covered cookie sheet at 350°F (177°C) for 50-60 minutes or until they are fully cooked and soft when pierced with a fork. Once done, remove them from the oven and cool for 10 minutes.
2. In a small bowl, combine all remaining ingredients except the pecans.
3. Cut the potatoes in half lengthwise, scooping out the flesh while leaving the skins intact. Using a potato masher or stand mixer, mash the potato flesh until smooth.
4. Gently combine the butter mixture with the whipped potatoes.
5. Spoon the mixture back into the potato skins, top with pecans, and bake on the cookie sheet for an additional 10 minutes until heated through.

VARIATIONS

Use an equal amount of maple syrup as a substitute for coconut sugar. Opt for ground coriander in place of cinnamon. Swap out the raisins for dried cranberries.

SERVING SUGGESTIONS

These delicious potatoes pair well with Zucchini Discs (p. 94) and Quick Nut Roast (p. 77) or with Sunny Burgers (p. 85) and Colorful Cucumber Salad (p. 121).

PLANNING AHEAD

These potatoes can be refrigerated and then reheated. Place in a covered casserole dish with 1/8-inch (0.3 cm) water on the bottom and bake at 300°F (149°C) for 30 minutes.

THANKSGIVING SWEET POTATOES

"Thy way, O God, is in the sanctuary: who is so great a God as our God?" Psalm 77:13

My husband, Kent, eagerly anticipates the holidays each year because this is one of his favorite dishes on the table. Of course, I sometimes make it just because!

◆

INGREDIENTS

1 can (40 oz./1.1 kg) sweet potatoes, drained

1/3 c. (45 g) pecan meal

1/3 c. (27 g) shredded coconut

1/3 c. (47 g) sorghum flour

1/4 c. (48 g) coconut sugar

1/4 c. (56 g) Butterless Butter (p. 150)

INSTRUCTIONS

1. Place sweet potatoes in a 9 x 9-inch (23 x 23-cm) baking dish. Set aside.
2. Combine remaining ingredients in a mixing bowl. Sprinkle over the top of the sweet potatoes.
3. Cover and bake at 350°F (177°C) for 30 minutes.

VARIATIONS

Chopped pecans may be used instead of pecan meal for added crunch.

SERVING SUGGESTIONS

As its name suggests, this dish appears on our Thanksgiving table every year. Use it as a side for a nice roast such as Holiday Tofu Roast (p. 78), with a cooked veggie like Glazed Beets (p. 93), and served with a salad like Aunt Greta's Green Salad (p. 109) for a true celebratory meal. You may even want to make some Perfect Pumpkin Pie (p. 221) for dessert!

PLANNING AHEAD

This dish can be made a few hours in advance and then warmed when ready to serve.

Salads

AUNT GRETA'S GREEN SALAD

"Fear thou not; for I am with thee: be not dismayed; for I am thy God: I will strengthen thee; yea, I will help thee; yea, I will uphold thee with the right hand of my righteousness." Isaiah 41:10

My Aunt Greta makes the best green salads! She made the salad for our wedding meal and is the go-to salad maker for family get-togethers. With her homegrown lettuce and innovative touches, such as adding crushed garlic to the dressing, her salads are consistently outstanding. Each salad shows Aunt Greta's thoughtfulness and kindness, characteristics she learned from the Great Teacher.

SALAD

4 c. (about 188 g) lettuce, chopped

1 c. (30 g) spinach, chopped

2 c. (50 g) microgreens, chopped

2-3 green onions, thinly sliced

Half of a cucumber, peeled and sliced

Half of a green bell pepper, diced

1/4 c. (30 g) pumpkin seeds, for garnish (optional)

DRESSING

1/3 c. (80 mL) avocado oil

1/4 c. (60 mL) lemon juice

1/2 tsp. (3 g) salt

INSTRUCTIONS

1. In a large serving bowl, combine all salad ingredients except the pumpkin seeds and mix together.
2. In a small, lidded jar, shake the dressing ingredients to combine.
3. Drizzle dressing over the salad just before serving to keep the greens crisp. Garnish with pumpkin seeds if desired.

VARIATIONS

Use the darkest green lettuce or mixed greens you can find or grow. Customize the salad with other in-season veggies that your family loves. Add different herbs to the dressing.

SERVING SUGGESTIONS

This salad pairs perfectly with any entree, baked Irish or sweet potatoes, and a fresh or frozen cooked vegetable for a great sit-down meal.

PLANNING AHEAD

You can prep the veggies several hours ahead, cover the bowl with plastic wrap, and refrigerate until ready to serve.

3 BEAN SALAD

"As thy days, so shall thy strength be." Deuteronomy 33:25

I love this colorful and flavor-filled salad! It's a high-protein dish that I pair with many meals.

SALAD

1 can (15 oz./425 g) green beans

1 can (15 oz./442 g) kidney beans

1 can (15 oz./425 g) chickpeas

1/2 c. (88 g) green bell pepper, diced

1/2 c. (50 g) celery, sliced

1/2 c. (75 g) onion, diced

DRESSING

4 Tbsp. (45 mL) avocado oil

4 Tbsp. (80 mL) lemon juice

1/2 tsp. (3 g) salt

INSTRUCTIONS

1. Drain the canned beans and add to a medium-sized serving bowl with remaining salad ingredients. Stir to combine.
2. Place dressing ingredients in a small jar and shake to combine.
3. Drizzle dressing over the salad and stir.
4. Chill for several hours to allow the flavors to meld together.

VARIATIONS

Choose different combinations of beans and include orange and yellow peppers to give more color to the dish.

SERVING SUGGESTIONS

This salad is a great companion to Grandma's Cabbage Borscht (p. 133) or Creamy German Potato Soup (p. 134), served with Auntie Joan's Baked Beans (p. 86) and Creamy Potato Salad (p. 125), plus Mom's Corn Bread (p. 42) on the side.

PLANNING AHEAD

This salad is ideal for preparing a day in advance, giving the flavors plenty of time to marinate.

BEET SALAD

"Yea, though I walk through the valley of the shadow of death, I will fear no evil: for thou art with me; thy rod and thy staff they comfort me." Psalm 23:4

This dish delivers the nutrients of beets in a fresh, bright salad.

SALAD

4 c. (600 g) beets *(cooked with 1/2 tsp./3 g salt, cooled and chopped)*

1/2-3/4 c. (75-113 g) onion, diced

DRESSING

1/3 c. (80 mL) avocado oil

1/4 c. (60 mL) lemon juice

1/2 tsp. (3 g) salt

2 Tbsp. (42 g) agave

INSTRUCTIONS

1. Combine the salad ingredients in a medium-sized serving bowl.
2. Place dressing ingredients in a small jar and shake to combine. Drizzle over salad and stir.

VARIATIONS

Add 1/2 cup (50 g) finely chopped celery to the salad for a pop of green.

SERVING SUGGESTIONS

This salad gives you one more delicious way to serve beets to your family. It's a colorful addition to any meal.

PLANNING AHEAD

This is a great salad to make in advance as you can make it completely and keep it refrigerated for several hours without changing the texture or taste of the salad.

SHREDDED CABBAGE SALAD

"Fear ye not, stand still, and see the salvation of the LORD, which he will shew to you to day." Exodus 14:13

I make sure we enjoy a generous salad—whether enhanced with special additions or kept simple—at least once a day, and this one is a typical selection! My kids love choosing the veggies and shaking up the dressing. Eating raw and fresh foods delights our taste buds and nourishes our bodies!

◆

SALAD

Half of a medium-sized head of cabbage, finely shredded

1/2 c. bright-colored bell peppers, diced

1/2 c. red onions, sliced in thin rings

DRESSING

1/3 c. (80 mL) avocado oil

1/4 c. (60 mL) lemon juice

1/2 tsp. (3 g) salt

INSTRUCTIONS

1. In a medium-sized serving bowl, toss the salad ingredients to combine.
2. Place dressing ingredients in a small jar and shake to combine. Drizzle over salad and stir.

VARIATIONS

Make this salad with only the cabbage and add 1–2 tablespoons (15–30 g) maple syrup to the dressing. Generously sprinkle with paprika before serving.

SERVING SUGGESTIONS

This salad is a versatile go-to option that pairs well with various main dishes. I serve it with any of the entrees in this book and add a cooked veggie of choice for a complete and wholesome everyday meal.

PLANNING AHEAD

This salad can be made an hour ahead, even with the dressing on it, without changing the texture.

CRUNCHY CARROT SALAD

"But thou, O LORD, art a shield for me; my glory, and the lifter up of mine head." Psalm 3:3

This vibrant salad reminds me of conversations with my friend Lena. She is like the carrots (emotionally nutritious), raisins (spiritually sweet), and pineapple (adding brightness to my life). Though one of us is from California and the other from Canada, Providence has woven our lives together, allowing us to support each other as wives, mothers, homeschool educators, and community teachers.

INGREDIENTS

4-6 carrots, finely grated

1 can (20 oz./567 g) crushed pineapple, undrained

1/4-1/2 c. (40-80 g) raisins

INSTRUCTIONS

1. Mix all ingredients together and enjoy!

VARIATIONS

Replace some or all of the raisins with dried cranberries.

SERVING SUGGESTIONS

Pair this salad with your favorite soup or entrée to brighten up the table. Try it with Saucy Soy Loaf (p.70) with a cooked veggie on the side or use it to accompany Creamy German Potato Soup (p. 134) with Eggless Salad Sandwich Spread (p. 142).

PLANNING AHEAD

This salad will keep its texture and taste even when made several hours before serving.

KATHY'S CONFETTI SALAD

"And it shall come to pass, that before they call, I will answer; and while they are yet speaking, I will hear."

Isaiah 65:24

Kathy and I have been friends for many years, but with the busyness of our lives, we have had few chances to spend time together. During the creation of this cookbook, God put her name in my mind as someone who could assist with the food styling for the photos. She proved to be an invaluable help with her remarkable creativity! Beyond the work, it was a wonderful opportunity to strengthen our friendship, transforming Kathy from a friend to my "sister of the heart."

SALAD

1 can (16 oz./453 g) corn, drained, or 2 c. (340 g) frozen corn, fully cooked and cooled

2 c. (400 g) cooked brown rice, cooled *(1 c./200 g dry rice cooked with 2 1/2 c./591 mL water for about 40 minutes)*

1/2 c. diced green pepper

1/4 c. (24 g) green onions, sliced, or 1/2 tsp. (1.2 g) onion powder

1 can (16 oz./360 g) black olives, drained and sliced

1 1/2 c. (300 g) tomatoes, diced

8 cherry tomatoes, halved, for garnish

DRESSING

3 Tbsp. (45 mL) avocado oil

3 Tbsp. (45 mL) lemon juice

2 Tbsp. (33 g) Bragg Liquid Aminos

2 Tbsp. (8 g) fresh parsley, minced, or 1 Tbsp. (2 g) parsley flakes

1/4 tsp. (0.8 g) garlic powder *(optional)*

INSTRUCTIONS

1. In a medium-sized bowl, combine all the salad ingredients except the tomatoes.
2. Place dressing ingredients in a small jar and shake to combine. Drizzle over salad and stir.
3. Stir in the tomatoes right before serving. Add the garnish of cherry tomatoes if desired.

VARIATIONS

Use different colors of bell peppers. Swap parsley for cilantro.

SERVING SUGGESTIONS

This salad is perfect for picnics and potlucks. Pair it with Mom's Navy Bean Soup (p. 138) and Toasty Oat Crackers (p. 49) for a colorful and satisfying lunch. For a hearty meal, team it up with Saucy Soy Loaf (p. 70) and Glazed Beets (p.93).

PLANNING AHEAD

This salad can be prepared several hours or even one day before serving. Add the tomatoes just before serving so they do not become watery.

COLORFUL CUCUMBER SALAD

"Thou shalt weep no more: he will be very gracious unto thee at the voice of thy cry; when he shall hear it, he will answer thee." Isaiah 30:19

What food captures the essence of summer better than a cucumber? Nothing beats a refreshing cucumber salad on a hot summer day, and this recipe is our family's all-time favorite during the summer months. When cucumbers are too large for making dill pickles, they're just the right size for this delightful salad!

◆

SALAD

6 c. (900 g) cucumbers, thinly sliced

1 small red onion, thinly sliced in rings

1/2 c. (30 g) fresh parsley, minced

DRESSING

1/3 c. (80 mL) avocado oil

1/4 c. (60 mL) lemon juice

1/2 tsp. (3 g) salt

INSTRUCTIONS

1. Combine the salad ingredients in a medium-sized mixing bowl.
2. Place dressing ingredients in a small jar and shake to combine. Drizzle over the salad and stir.

VARIATIONS

Increase the color and flavor of this salad by adding 1 cup (200 g) halved cherry tomatoes. Use 4 green onions instead of the red onion.

SERVING SUGGESTIONS

This cool, refreshing, and colorful salad is an excellent addition to many meals. Serve it with Mac and Cheese Bake (p. 62) with a side of steamed peas, or with Sunny Burgers (p. 85), Creamy Dilly Potatoes (p. 97), and veggies.

PLANNING AHEAD

This salad is best made and eaten right away. Cucumbers have such a high water content that if you make this up several hours in advance, they will lose a large portion of their water.

GET YOU STARTED KALE SALAD

"I will instruct thee and teach thee in the way which thou shalt go: I will guide thee with mine eye." Psalm 32:8

I can picture the many crisp September mornings when Courtney and Luke enjoyed this kale salad for breakfast before heading off to community college classes. Baby Elizabeth would occasionally crawl out of bed in time to "beg" for a share. Happy memories together!

◆

SALAD

1 bunch kale, washed, ribbed, and finely chopped

1 can (15 oz./442 g) kidney beans, drained

1 can (15 oz./338 g) black olives, sliced

DRESSING

1/3 c. (80 mL) avocado oil

1/4 c. (60 mL) lemon juice

3/4 tsp. (5 g) salt

INSTRUCTIONS

1. Combine the salad ingredients in a large mixing bowl.
2. Place dressing ingredients in a small jar and shake to combine. Drizzle over salad and stir.

VARIATIONS

Add your favorite salad ingredients to add an extra splash of color to this salad. My favorites include sliced onions, diced bright-colored sweet peppers, pumpkin seeds, and hemp hearts. I sometimes use different dressings, such as my Avocado Sauce (p. 169). I have also made a lovely fruity salad by omitting the black olives and kidney beans and adding 1 tablespoon (21 g) honey to the dressing and mixing apple cubes and toasted chopped almonds in with the kale.

SERVING SUGGESTIONS

This salad delivers the combined power of raw greens and healthy protein. Add Sunflower Crackers (p. 50) or Courtney's Crackers (p. 53) for a great lunch. For a hearty meal, team it up with Grandma Marge's Potatoes (p. 101), cooked green beans, and Quick Burgers (p. 82).

PLANNING AHEAD

This salad may be eaten immediately or stored in the refrigerator for a few hours to one day.

CREAMY POTATO SALAD

"Be not wise in thine own eyes: fear the LORD, and depart from evil. It shall be health to thy navel, and marrow to thy bones." Proverbs 3:7–8

Growing up with traditional potato salad, I had to experiment for a while to create a plant-based version I truly enjoyed. I love serving this salad to family and friends. Empty bowls tell their own success stories!

INGREDIENTS

5 large potatoes, peeled

4 celery stalks, diced

1 can (16 oz./360 g) black olives, diced

1/2 c. (112 g) dill pickles, diced

1/2 c. (48 g) green onions, thinly sliced

4–6 radishes, thinly sliced

2 c. (460 g) Plant-Based Mayo (p. 174)

INSTRUCTIONS

1. Peel potatoes and place in a large saucepan with 1 inch (2.5 cm) salted water. Boil 30-44 minutes, or until the potatoes are soft. Drain off the excess water. Cool and then dice the potatoes.
2. Place diced potatoes in a medium-sized bowl. Add the remaining ingredients and stir to combine.
3. Chill well and garnish with a sprinkle of paprika, if desired, before serving.

VARIATIONS

Add 1/4 cup (44 g) diced red bell pepper for extra color. Use green olives to replace all or part of the black olives.

SERVING SUGGESTIONS

This salad is great picnic food! Couple it with Auntie Joan's Baked Beans (p. 86) and Aunt Greta's Green Salad (p. 109) for a yummy picnic lunch!

PLANNING AHEAD

This salad can be made several hours before serving.

TACO SALAD

"Come unto me, all ye that labour and are heavy laden, and I will give you rest." Matthew 11:28

It's picnic time! When you need a quick and satisfying dish, consider stirring up this vibrant and hearty taco salad. It's my go-to solution for busy days that leave me exhausted and hungry, and it's become a family favorite.

◆

SALAD

4-6 c. (720 g-1 kg) cooked kidney or pinto beans, drained well

4 c. (188 g) lettuce, shredded

2 medium tomatoes, diced

1 can (16 oz./360 g) black olives, sliced

1 green bell pepper, diced

1/2 c. bright-colored bell pepper, diced

1/2 c. (48 g) green onions, thinly sliced

1 avocado, sliced, for garnish

8 cherry tomatoes, halved, for garnish

DRESSING

1-2 Tbsp. (3-5 g) taco seasoning

2-3 c. (460-690 g) Plant-Based Mayo (p. 174) to achieve desired consistency

INSTRUCTIONS

1. Place beans and veggies (excluding avocado and tomatoes) in a serving bowl and stir to combine.
2. Use a fork to combine the mayo and taco seasoning.
3. Just before serving, add the dressing to the salad. Garnish with avocados and tomatoes and serve.

VARIATIONS

Add 1 cucumber to the salad for another dimension of crunch. Decrease the lettuce and add microgreens to still have 4 cups (188 g). Try using different types of beans. My favorites for this salad are kidney and pinto, but feel free to try a mixture of others!

SERVING SUGGESTIONS

This makes a great meal by itself. Top it off with corn chips and salsa.

PLANNING AHEAD

The veggies in this salad can be prepared in advance; add the dressing and garnishes just before serving.

WONDERFUL WILD RICE SALAD

"Fear not: for they that be with us are more than they that be with them." 2 Kings 6:16

This salad is fun to make with children. Let them pick their favorite colors and veggies to add. It's a fun and interactive way to involve them in the kitchen!

◆

SALAD

1 c. (185 g) uncooked wild rice

1/2 tsp. (3 g) salt

1 c. (150 g) carrots, diced

1 c. (100 g) celery, diced

1 c. (325 g) cauliflower, small pieces

1 c. (175 g) broccoli, small pieces

1/2 c. (88 g) green bell pepper, diced

1/2 c. (88 g) bright-colored bell pepper, diced

1/2 c. (58 g) radishes, thinly sliced

1/2 c. (75 g) purple onion, minced

1 c. (112 g) walnuts, coarsely chopped

1 can (16 oz./360 g) black olives, drained and sliced

DRESSING

2/3 c. (160 mL) avocado oil

1/2 c. (120 mL) lemon juice

1 tsp. (6 g) salt

INSTRUCTIONS

1. In a 5-6 quart (6 L) pot, bring 5 cups (1.2 L) water to a boil.
2. When water boils, add the wild rice and 1/2 teaspoon (3 g) salt. Cover with the lid slightly cocked to allow some steam to escape and simmer for 1 hour. The rice is cooked when most of the rice bursts open and turns white. By then, the excess water should have evaporated. This will yield about 3-4 cups of rice. Set aside to cool.
3. Mix the remaining salad ingredients in a large serving bowl. Add the cooled rice and stir to combine.
4. Place dressing ingredients in a small jar and shake to combine. Drizzle over salad and stir.

VARIATIONS

This salad brings together a variety of flavors and colors. Feel free to replace some wild rice with either brown or white rice. Customize the salad by adding your family's favorite veggies. Try using pecans instead of walnuts.

SERVING SUGGESTIONS

This salad pairs well with most meals where you want a heartier salad. I especially like to pair it with soups and sandwiches. One of my favorite combinations with this salad is Creamy German Potato Soup (p. 134) and Garden Tomato Sandwich Spread (p. 145).

PLANNING AHEAD

This salad is a perfect one to make a few hours to one day ahead. The veggies will stay crisp and delicious.

Soups
&
Sandwiches

GRANDMA'S CABBAGE BORSCHT

"And even to your old age I am he; and even to hoar hairs will I carry you: I have made, and I will bear; even I will carry, and will deliver you." Isaiah 46:4

My mother's mom, my Grandma Funk, was an excellent cook. I fondly recall her white enamel pot, decorated with a simple red line around the top, filled with this soup. There's nothing quite like a bowl of soup at Grandma's house. Once I got my driver's license, I had the privilege of taking Grandma to the city to buy groceries all by myself for several years. Those were special days of shopping together, talking, hearing the stories of her life, and often ending a beautiful day with a bowl of borscht.

◆

INGREDIENTS

1 small head of cabbage, finely shredded

4-6 potatoes, diced

1 medium onion, diced

3 garlic cloves, minced

1 can (28 oz./794 g) tomatoes, diced or petite diced

1 can (6 oz./170 g) tomato paste

3 Tbsp. (45 mL) avocado oil

1 handful fresh dill or 1 Tbsp. dried dill

1 Tbsp. (18 g) salt

INSTRUCTIONS

1. Fill a 6-quart (6 L) heavy-bottomed pot half full of water.
2. Add the ingredients and cook together until the veggies are soft, about 30–45 minutes.

VARIATIONS

Add 1 cup (150 g) raw shredded beets and 1 cup (150 g) raw shredded carrots for added nutrition and color.

SERVING SUGGESTIONS

This soup is an excellent start for a fantastic meal. Pair it with Eggless Salad Sandwich Spread (p. 142), Tuna Salad Sandwich Spread (p.141), or some Garden Tomato Sandwich Spread (p. 145) on your favorite gluten-free bread or crackers, along with a fresh veggie platter and a bowl of Creamy Cucumber Dip (p. 166) for an excellent lunch.

PLANNING AHEAD

This soup tastes best hot, freshly made, or warmed up a few days later. You can put it in airtight containers and freeze it for up to one month. Allow time to thaw before heating up for another excellent meal!

CREAMY GERMAN POTATO SOUP

"And they that know thy name will put their trust in thee: for thou, LORD,
hast not forsaken them that seek thee." Psalm 9:10

This is a cherished family recipe that has been passed down through the generations. My mother, grandmother, great-grandmother, and possibly even my great-great-grandmother made it—except for the plant-based cream! They were all farmers who milked cows and cooked nearly everything with cream. The star anise in this soup adds an incredible dimension of flavor.

SOUP

4 tsp. (24 g) salt

3-5 bay leaves

2-3 whole star anise

1 medium onion, minced

5 stalks celery, thinly sliced

2 1/2-3 lbs. (1.1-1.4 kg) red potatoes, peeled and cubed

CREAM

1 c. (237 mL) water

1/2 c. (64 g) cashews

1/2 tsp. (3 g) salt

1/2 tsp. (1.2 g) onion powder

2 Tbsp. (16 g) cornstarch

INSTRUCTIONS

1. Fill a 6-quart (6 L)pot half full of water. Boil the water and add the soup seasonings.
2. Add the onion and celery and boil for a few more minutes before adding the potatoes so that they will all finish cooking at the same time.
3. Cook the soup for about 30 minutes or until the vegetables are soft.
4. Place cream ingredients in a blender and blend until very creamy.
5. Add the cream to the soup and bring it just to a boil before removing from heat. Serve immediately.

VARIATIONS

Add 1 small grated carrot to the potatoes for an added splash of color.

SERVING SUGGESTIONS

This soup is best served hot. It makes a great meal when paired with Garden Tomato Sandwich Spread (p. 145), Eggless Salad Sandwich Spread (p. 142), or Tuna Salad Sandwich Spread (p. 141) on your favorite gluten-free bread or crackers. Add a raw veggie plate or a salad to round out your meal. I especially like to pair it with Wonderful Wild Rice Salad (p. 129) or Three Bean Salad (p. 110).

PLANNING AHEAD

This soup can be refrigerated for 4-5 days. The flavors of the herbs will intensify somewhat during refrigeration.

MOM'S MINESTRONE SOUP

"I laid me down and slept; I awaked; for the LORD sustained me." Psalm 3:5

I often prepare a large pot of soup at the beginning of the week, ensuring I have several quick-prep meals ready to go. My family frequently requests this soup.

◆

INGREDIENTS

3 c. (420 g) mixed dried beans of choice (pinto, great northern, kidney, black, lima, etc.)

1/2 c. (120 mL) avocado oil

1 large onion, diced

2 garlic cloves, minced

1 1/2 c. (150 g) celery, sliced

2 c. (178 g) cabbage, shredded

2 c. (300 g) zucchini, diced

2 cans (28 oz./794 g each) diced or petite diced tomatoes, salted

4 tsp. (24 g) salt

1/4 c. (15 g) fresh parsley, minced

INSTRUCTIONS

1. Wash and drain beans. Pour 3 quarts (3 L) water into a large heavy-bottomed pot. Add salt.
2. Bring salted water to a boil. Add the beans, cover, and remove from heat. Let stand for 15-60 minutes.
3. Strain off the water and add 3 more quarts (3 L) of water.
4. Bring to a boil, cover, and simmer for 1 1/2 hours or until tender.
5. In a skillet, sauté onions, garlic, and celery in oil for 10 minutes, stirring frequently. Add cabbage and zucchini and cook for an additional 10 minutes. Add this mixture to the beans.
6. Add tomatoes, salt, and parsley. Cover and simmer for 45 minutes or until all vegetables are soft. Stir frequently to prevent scorching. Adjust salt and water to achieve the desired taste and texture.

VARIATIONS

Involve your children by letting them choose the combination of beans for this soup—it all tastes great and will look beautiful! You can also add some of your favorite gluten-free pasta to the soup during the last 20 minutes of cooking.

SERVING SUGGESTIONS

This hearty soup can be a meal in a bowl. Pair it with Courtney's Crackers (p. 53) and a veggie tray with Creamy Cucumber Dip (p. 166) for a satisfying meal.

PLANNING AHEAD

This soup stores well for up to one week in the refrigerator. It can also be frozen for up to one month in an airtight container. Allow time for thawing before warming and serving.

MOM'S
NAVY BEAN SOUP

"I will sing unto the LORD, because he hath dealt bountifully with me." Psalm 13:6

Soups like this one serve as foundational elements for a meal. We eagerly anticipate the winter months when our local church hosts a monthly soup supper. It's a gathering with an array of soups to savor along with music, singing, and games. The friendships nurtured over a bowl of soup are profound!

Thanks to Darrell and Tami for hosting these fellowship-rich suppers.

Many of our lasting friendships were established and strengthened over a bowl of soup.

◆

INGREDIENTS

2 c. (320 g) dry navy beans

8 c. (1.9 L) water

2 tsp. (12 g) salt

3 carrots, diced

3 celery stalks, thinly sliced

1 medium onion, diced

3 Tbsp. (45 mL) avocado oil

1 can (28 oz./794 g) tomatoes, diced or petite diced, salted

2 Tbsp. dried parsley

INSTRUCTIONS

1. Bring water to a boil. Add beans and remove from heat. Allow to soak for 30 minutes or longer. Drain and rinse the beans.
2. Add 8 more cups (1.9 L) water and salt to the beans. Return to heat and keep them boiling until they are nearly cooked.
3. Add remaining veggies and cook until all are tender. Add more salt or water to achieve desired consistency.

VARIATIONS

Add extra color to this soup by mixing the navy beans with other beans.

SERVING SUGGESTIONS

This soup is versatile and delicious, making it a great companion to various veggies and dishes. I enjoy it with Toasted Cheese Sandwiches (p. 146) or with Garlic Butter (p. 153) on gluten-free bread or crackers.

PLANNING AHEAD

This soup stays fresh in the refrigerator for 4–5 days and freezes nicely in an airtight container for up to one month. Remember to thaw it before reheating.

TUNA SALAD SANDWICH SPREAD

"The LORD is good, a strong hold in the day of trouble; and he knoweth them that trust in him." Nahum 1:7

I've never had tuna, so I can't vouch for its authentic flavor, but this spread is certainly delicious!

INGREDIENTS

1 can (15 oz./425 g) chickpeas, drained

1/4 c. (58 g) Plant-Based Mayo (p. 174)

2 celery stalks, sliced

1 Tbsp. (5 g) nutritional yeast flakes

1/2 tsp. (1 g) vegetable seasoning (I prefer Vegit)

1/2 tsp. (1 g) smoked paprika

1/2 tsp. (1.5 g) garlic powder

2 Tbsp. (33 g) Bragg Liquid Aminos

1/2 tsp. (1 g) celery seed, ground

Salt to taste

2 Tbsp. (12 g) green onions, thinly sliced, for garnish

INSTRUCTIONS

1. Place all ingredients except green onions in a food processor with the blade attachment and blend to the desired texture.
2. Garnish with onions and serve chilled.

VARIATIONS

Experiment with various beans and seasonings to find your favorite combination!

SERVING SUGGESTIONS

This pairs well with Toasty Oat Crackers (p. 49), your favorite gluten-free bread, as a dip for chips, or along with Creamy German Potato Soup (p. 134) or Kathy's Confetti Salad (p. 118) for a delicious lunch.

PLANNING AHEAD

Refrigerate this spread for increased flavor blending; it keeps well for several days in an airtight container in the refrigerator.

EGGLESS SALAD SANDWICH SPREAD

"I give unto them eternal life; and they shall never perish, neither shall any man pluck them out of my hand." John 10:28

I remember attending my great-grandmother's birthday parties, where we would enjoy delicate egg salad sandwiches with no crust rolled up like jelly rolls. They were exquisite! Now, I have a plant-based version that is tasty, packed with protein, and doesn't support a "fowl" industry. Plus, it's cholesterol-free, allowing me to enjoy a free-flowing circulatory system.

INGREDIENTS

12.3 oz. (349 g) soft or firm silken tofu

1 1/2 tsp. (3.6 g) onion powder

1/4 tsp. (1 g) garlic powder

1 Tbsp. (17 g) Bragg Liquid Aminos

1 Tbsp. (4 g) fresh parsley, minced

1 1/2 tsp. (1.8 g) McKay's Chicken Style Seasoning

1 Tbsp. (5 g) nutritional yeast flakes

1/4-1/2 c. (68-115 g) Tofu Mayo (p. 174)

INSTRUCTIONS

1. Place ingredients in a stand mixer with a beater attachment and combine thoroughly.
2. Chill and serve.

VARIATIONS

Customize your spread by experimenting with combinations of your favorite herbs.

SERVING SUGGESTIONS

This spread tastes great on your favorite gluten-free bread, rice cakes, or Toasty Oat Crackers (p. 49) and topped with your favorite microgreens. It also makes a lovely dip for crackers, veggies, etc. Team it up with soup or salad for a great meal.

PLANNING AHEAD

This spread is perfect for preparing a day or two in advance. Allowing it to sit in an airtight container in the refrigerator for a couple of days will enhance the flavors.

GARDEN TOMATO SANDWICH SPREAD

"The angel of the LORD encampeth round about them that fear him, and delivereth them." Psalm 34:7

Several years ago, I went on a camping trip along the backwaters of the Mississippi River with my husband and six children. Our eldest daughter had just returned from a summer spent cooking for a Christian camp, and we were happy to have the whole family together again. I served this spread on our first evening and watched it disappear as we talked and laughed. It was gratifying to clean up the empty bowls after supper, knowing that I had served something that was loved by all of my family.

◆

WET INGREDIENTS

1 can (28 oz./794 g) tomatoes, whole or diced

2 Tbsp. (33 g) Bragg Liquid Aminos

1/2 c. (128 g) almond butter

1 tsp. (6 g) salt

DRY INGREDIENTS

1 medium onion, diced

1 c. (100 g) celery, thinly sliced

1 c. (112 g) almond flour

1 c. (140 g) sorghum flour

1 c. (160 g) tapioca starch

2 Tbsp. (30 g) psyllium husk powder

TOPPING

2 bay leaves

1/2 c. (118 mL) hot water

INSTRUCTIONS

1. Place wet ingredients in a blender and blend to combine.
2. Place dry ingredients in a stand mixer with a beater attachment and combine thoroughly. Mix in the wet ingredients.
3. Place in a greased 9 x 9-inch (23 x 23-cm) casserole dish and cover with water and bay leaves.
4. Bake, uncovered, at 350°F (177°C) for 1 1/2 hours. Once cooled, use the beater attachment on a stand mixer to break the loaf into small pieces.
5. Add Plant-Based Mayonnaise (p. 174), sliced celery, sliced black olives, diced onions, and sliced dill pickles to taste and until the mixture reaches the desired consistency.

VARIATIONS

This sandwich spread is easy to customize to the taste preferences of your family. Experiment with combinations of the suggested add-ins when you mix the loaf with Plant-Based Mayonnaise (p. 174) or try some new additions of your own!

SERVING SUGGESTIONS

This spread complements Creamy German Potato Soup (p. 134), your favorite raw veggies, and Toasty Oat Crackers (p.49) for a delicious light meal.

PLANNING AHEAD

This sandwich spread can be frozen for 1-2 months after baking. You can also prepare it several days in advance, store it in sealed containers in the refrigerator, and mix it with Plant-Based Mayonnaise (p. 174) and other additions a few hours before serving.

TOASTED CHEESE SANDWICHES

"Behold, God is my salvation; I will trust, and not be afraid: for the LORD JEHOVAH is my strength and my song; he also is become my salvation." Isaiah 12:2

These sandwiches pair well with soup and are enhanced by the delightful flavor of dill. Another special treat and family favorite!

◆

INGREDIENTS

1 c. (237 mL) water

3/4 c. (96 g) cashews

2 Tbsp. (24 g) sesame seeds

1 1/4 tsp. (8 g) salt (to taste)

1/4 tsp. (0.8 g) garlic powder

1/4 c. (20 g) quick oats

2 tsp. (5 g) onion powder

1/4 tsp. (0.3 g) dill (optional)

3 Tbsp. (15 g) nutritional yeast flakes

1/2 c. (87 g) pimentos

2 Tbsp. (30 g) lemon juice

INSTRUCTIONS

1. Combine ingredients in a blender and blend until smooth.
2. Cook the mixture in a heavy-bottomed saucepan until thick, whisking constantly.
3. Spread on slices of your preferred gluten-free bread and assemble into a sandwich.
4. Place on a cookie sheet and toast at 375°F (191°C) to your desired level of toastiness.

VARIATIONS

Use blanched almonds or Brazil nuts instead of cashews for a different flavor and consistency.

SERVING SUGGESTIONS

Pair these sandwiches with a salad of your choice and some mixed nuts for a light meal. I also love them with a bowl of Grandma's Cabbage Borscht (p. 133).

PLANNING AHEAD

This cheese can be stored in an airtight container in the refrigerator for several days.

Butters, Cheeses, & Gravy

BUTTERLESS BUTTER

"Verily, verily, I say unto you, He that heareth my word, and believeth on him that sent Me, hath everlasting life, and shall not come into condemnation; but is passed from death unto life." John 5:24

I love this butter because it allows me to craft a spread with ingredients I recognize, avoiding hard-to-pronounce additives.

◆

INGREDIENTS

1 1/2 c. (360 g) refined coconut oil, warmed to liquid

1/2 c. (120 mL) Homemade Soy Milk (p.23), unsweetened

1/4 c. (60 mL) avocado or light olive oil

1 Tbsp. (15 mL) lemon juice

2 tsp. (10 g) liquid lecithin

2-inch (5 cm) carrot chunk, diced

INSTRUCTIONS

1. Place ingredients in a blender and blend for 1 minute.
2. Pour into a container and chill until the butter has set (I like to use silicone molds so I can easily pop the chilled butter out and serve it without a container.)

VARIATIONS

Experiment with different oils and plant-based milks to create the perfect butter for you.

SERVING SUGGESTIONS

This butter can be used wherever you typically use butter—on bread, muffins, crackers, and baked potatoes or for baking pies and cookies.

PLANNING AHEAD

This butter will keep refrigerated for 3-4 weeks, so it's easy to make a large batch and always have butter on hand!

GARLIC BUTTER

"For God so loved the world, that he gave his only begotten Son, that whosoever believeth in him should not perish, but have everlasting life." John 3:16

What's better than garlic bread with your favorite pasta dishes or a hot bowl of soup?
I love garlic butter that doesn't contain butter!

◆

CORNMEAL

2 c. (473 mL) water

1/4 tsp. (1.5 g) salt

2/3 c. (107 g) cornmeal, finely ground

BUTTER

1 c. (237 mL) water

1/2 c. (64 g) cashews

4-6 whole garlic cloves

1 Tbsp. (15 mL) lemon juice

1/2 tsp. (0.5 g) dill weed

2 tsp. (5 g) onion powder

1 1/2 tsp. (9 g) salt

INSTRUCTIONS

1. Bring water and salt to boil in a small saucepan. When the water boils, whisk in cornmeal.
2. Reduce heat to simmer and allow to cook for 3-5 minutes.
3. Add cooked cornmeal and remaining ingredients until combined. It will thicken as it cools.

VARIATIONS

For a special occasion, enjoy thick slices of your favorite gluten-free bread generously spread with Garlic Butter. Cut bread into 2-inch (5 cm) wide sticks and toast in the oven until the edges are crisp. This butter is also delicious on fresh rolls!

SERVING SUGGESTIONS

This garlic butter makes an excellent spread for breads and rolls to be teamed up with your favorite soups, salads, or pasta dishes. I especially love it when toasted on bread and served with Grandma's Cabbage Borscht (p. 133) or Jonathan's Manicotti (p. 65) with a large salad.

PLANNING AHEAD

The butter can be made in advance and will store well in the refrigerator for 4-5 days.

JUDY'S CHEESE

"For the LORD God is a sun and shield: the LORD will give grace and glory: no good thing will he withhold from them that walk uprightly." Psalm 84:11

This cheese brings back fond memories of my dear friend Judy K. We shared countless meals and laughter for nearly 25 years, living just minutes apart. Our husbands also enjoyed each other's company, and time always went by too quickly when we were together. Now, with greater distance between us, phone calls keep us connected. When we do get to see each other, it feels like a piece of heaven.

◆

THICKENER

3/4 c. (177 mL) water

1 Tbsp. (4 g) agar agar powder

CHEESE

1/2 c. (118 mL) water

1 c. (128 g) cashews

1/4 c. (20 g) nutritional yeast flakes

1 1/2 tsp. (9 g) salt

1 tsp. (2.4 g) onion powder

1/4 tsp. (0.8 g) garlic powder

1/4 c. (60 mL) lemon juice

INSTRUCTIONS

1. In a small saucepan, bring water to a boil. Use a sturdy whisk to mix in the agar agar and cook for 2 minutes on low heat, stirring constantly.
2. Place remaining ingredients in a blender and blend for 2 minutes until creamy.
3. Add the hot water and agar agar mixture and blend on high speed for 1 minute.
4. Pour into containers. I choose containers that are rectangular with a depth of 3/4–1 1/2 inches (1.9–3.8 cm).
5. Refrigerate for several hours. Slice and serve.

VARIATIONS

Use almonds or Brazil nuts in place of cashews. Add 1/4 cup (43 g) diced pimentos to create a yellow cheese, as pictured. Experiment with your favorite herbs, fruits, nuts, etc., to make a delicious cheese of your own! Here are two of my favorite cheeses:

· Olive Cheese: Between steps 3 and 4, fold in 1/2 cup (90 g) diced black and/or green olives. Continue on to step 5.
· Dilly White Cheese: Between steps 3 and 4, fold in 1 tablespoon (3 g) dried dill weed or 3 tablespoons (9 g) finely chopped fresh dill weed. Continue on to step 5.

SERVING SUGGESTIONS

These cheeses go beautifully as an appetizer with fresh crackers and fruit. Try them on sandwiches or with your favorite soup!

PLANNING AHEAD

This recipe refrigerates well and can be stored for 2–3 days before your planned serving time.

PIMENTO CHEESE SAUCE

"Be strong and of a good courage..." Joshua 1:6

This cheese is smooth, creamy, and incredibly delicious! I grow my own pimentos just for this recipe. I wash, seed, slice, and freeze them in 1/2-cup (87 g) servings for their fantastic flavor in this sauce. Of course, canned ones from the store work well, too!

◆

INGREDIENTS

4 c. (946 mL) water, divided

1/2 c. (87 g) pimentos

1/2 c. (40 g) nutritional yeast flakes

1 Tbsp. (18 g) salt

1 tsp. (2.4 g) onion powder

1/2 tsp. (1.5 g) garlic powder

6 Tbsp. (48 g) cornstarch

1/2 c. (64 g) cashews

3 Tbsp. (45 mL) lemon juice

INSTRUCTIONS

1. Boil 2 cups (473 mL) water in a small saucepan.
2. Place the ingredients, including an additional 2 cups (473 mL) water, in a blender and blend for 2 minutes.
3. Add the mixture to the boiling water and whisk until it boils.

VARIATIONS

Try almonds instead of cashews. Omit pimentos if a white cheese is desired.

SERVING SUGGESTIONS

This cheese is excellent on haystacks, cooked bean dishes, drizzled over steamed broccoli, or as a dip for corn chips.

PLANNING AHEAD

This cheese is best served hot and fresh. You can blend up the ingredients and store them in an airtight container for several days before cooking.

CREAMY CASHEW GRAVY

"He giveth power to the faint; and to them that have no might he increaseth strength." Isaiah 40:29

This mild gravy goes with nearly everything. Savory, creamy, delicious, and nutritious are all great descriptions for it! This cashew gravy has been my personal favorite for decades.

INGREDIENTS

3 c. (710 mL) water, divided

1 c. (128 g) cashews

3 Tbsp. (24 g) cornstarch

2 Tbsp. (33 g) Bragg Liquid Aminos

2 tsp. (5 g) onion powder

1 tsp. (6 g) salt

INSTRUCTIONS

1. In a medium-sized heavy-bottomed saucepan, boil 2 cups (473 mL) water.
2. Place the ingredients, including 1 cup (237 mL) water, in a blender and blend until smooth and creamy.
3. Pour the blended ingredients into the boiling water and whisk constantly until mixture boils.

VARIATIONS

Use blanched and peeled almonds instead of cashews if you want a very white gravy. Try 1/2 teaspoon (1 g) ground celery seed instead of the Bragg. You can omit the Bragg from the cashew version of this gravy for a whiter color and increase the salt by 1/4 teaspoon (1.5 g).

SERVING SUGGESTIONS

This gravy is versatile, tasty, and nutritious. It works well over baked or steamed potatoes, drizzled over Cashew Nut Loaf (p. 69), or with Curtis's Oat Burgers (p. 81).

PLANNING AHEAD

This gravy is best served hot. Mix the dry ingredients ahead of time in an airtight container to save time.

SUE'S HOMESTYLE GRAVY

"I have set the LORD always before me: because he is at my right hand, I shall not be moved." Psalm 16:8

This gravy, a favorite of my husband's, was generously shared by my dear sister-in-law Sue. It has been adapted to be gluten-free but keeps its wonderful flavor, a reminder of Sue and her fantastic cooking!

◆

INGREDIENTS

4 c. (946 mL) water

2 Tbsp. (33 g) Bragg Liquid Aminos

1 tsp. (1.2 g) McKay's Chicken Style Seasoning

2 Tbsp. (10 g) nutritional yeast flakes

Dash of thyme

3 Tbsp. (45 mL) avocado oil

1 small onion, diced

1/4 c. (35 g) sorghum flour

1/3 c. (43 g) cornstarch

INSTRUCTIONS

1. In a measuring glass, whisk the water and seasonings to mix.
2. In a medium-sized skillet, sauté the oil and onion until soft.
3. Add flour and cornstarch, stirring constantly until flour browns.
4. Pour the seasoned water into the flour mixture and stir constantly until it boils. The gravy will thicken as it cools.

VARIATIONS

Use McKay's Beef Style Seasoning and omit the thyme.

SERVING SUGGESTIONS

This gravy is perfect over mashed potatoes, Curtis's Oat Burgers (p.81), or Quick Nut Roast (p. 77). This is also my favorite gravy to pour over Better Biscuits (p. 45) for a savory breakfast.

PLANNING AHEAD

This gravy is best served hot and fresh, but it can be stored in an airtight container in the refrigerator for several days and reheated before serving.

Condiments & Dips

COURTNEY'S HUMMUS

"I will not fail thee, nor forsake thee." Joshua 1:5

Courtney, our eldest daughter, is happily married and a loving mother to five beautiful children. It brings me joy to visit them and savor her delicious food. While some dishes reflect the taste of my cooking, others showcase her own culinary skills. This hummus is one such creation. They say a daughter is the little girl who grows up to be your friend, and that's certainly true in our case. We've shared countless hours in the kitchen, and I am grateful for her friendship and culinary expertise.

◆

INGREDIENTS

4 c. (720 g) cooked beans, drained (kidney, pinto, chickpeas, etc.)

1/2 c. (120 mL) avocado oil

1/3-1/2 c. (80-120 mL) lemon juice

1 tsp. (2 g) ground paprika

1 tsp. (2 g) ground cumin

1-2 garlic cloves or 1/2 tsp. (1.5 g) garlic powder

1 tsp. (6 g) salt, to taste

Water

INSTRUCTIONS

1. Place all ingredients in a food processor with the blade attachment and blend until smooth.
2. Add water as needed until hummus achieves your preferred consistency.

VARIATIONS

Experiment with various beans to create a range of colors. For a lovely plating option, serve the hummus in a hollowed-out bell pepper (remove the stem and seeds, leaving the pepper intact).

SERVING SUGGESTIONS

This hummus pairs nicely with corn chips, Toasty Oat Crackers (p. 49), and a tray of mixed veggies for dipping. Enjoy it with a bowl of Grandma's Cabbage Borscht (p. 133) or Creamy German Potato Soup (p.134). Need a quick lunch or picnic? Pair hummus with your choice of chips, veggies, or crackers. Add Wonderful Wild Rice Salad (p. 129) or Kathy's Confetti Salad (p. 118) for a great meal.

PLANNING AHEAD

This can be made a day or two in advance and refrigerated, which allows the flavors to meld together. It's best if not frozen.

CREAMY CUCUMBER DIP

"Fear not: for I have redeemed thee, I have called thee by thy name; thou art mine." Isaiah 43:1

Cucumbers are a summer garden highlight for my family. This dip perfectly captures their mild and delicious flavor. If it weren't against the "rules," I would eat it by the spoonful!

INGREDIENTS

12.3 oz. (349 g) soft or firm silken tofu

1/2 c. (118 mL) water

3 Tbsp. (45 mL) lemon juice

1/4 c. (85 g) honey

1/2 tsp. (1.5 g) garlic powder

1/2 Tbsp. (3 g) onion powder

1/4 c. (38 g) sweet onion or (24 g) green onions

1/2 tsp. (2 g) celery salt

1/2 tsp. (0.4 g) dried basil

2 tsp. (12 g) salt

Half of 1 cucumber, washed and peeled

1 avocado (optional)

INSTRUCTIONS

1. Place all ingredients in a blender and blend until smooth.
2. Chill and serve.

VARIATIONS

Experiment with your favorite herbs to create a personalized dressing!

SERVING SUGGESTIONS

This can be used as a delicious salad dressing for Aunt Greta's Green Salad (p. 109). It is also delicious as a veggie dip. You may wish to reduce the water to create a more dip-like consistency.

PLANNING AHEAD

This dressing will store in an airtight container in the refrigerator for several days.

AVOCADO SAUCE

"Be not afraid, only believe." Mark 5:36

I'm not a huge fan of avocados, but I absolutely love this sauce!

◆

INGREDIENTS

2 avocados

1/2 c. (64 g) cashews

1/3 c. (80 mL) lemon juice

1 Tbsp. (6 g) onion powder

1 1/2 tsp. (9 g) salt

1/4 tsp. (0.8 g) garlic powder

1 3/4 c. (414 mL) water

INSTRUCTIONS

1. Halve the avocados and scoop the avocado meat into the blender.
2. Add all other ingredients to the blender and blend until smooth.

VARIATIONS

Use blanched almonds instead of cashews.

SERVING SUGGESTIONS

This sauce is fantastic as a dip for corn chips with refried beans and salsa. It makes a great salad dressing for your green salads or as a dip for veggies. This is the perfect dressing for Get-You-Started Kale Salad (p. 122).

PLANNING AHEAD

This sauce is best when served immediately to preserve the lovely green color of the avocados.

ELIZABETH'S PASTA SAUCE

"The eternal God is thy refuge, and underneath are the everlasting arms..." Deuteronomy 33:27

Our daughter Elizabeth created this recipe, and we all love it! She enjoys making meals for our family and loves to bake cookies. It is rewarding to see her experimenting in the kitchen and creating new recipes!

INGREDIENTS

1 medium onion, diced

4 garlic cloves

3 Tbsp. (45 mL) avocado oil

3 1/2 c. (868 g) tomato sauce

1/2 c. (132 g) tomato paste

2 tsp. (12 g) salt

3 Tbsp. (63 g) honey

1 tsp. (2 g) Italian seasoning

1/8 tsp. (0.4 g) chili powder

1 tsp. (1 g) dried oregano

3/4 c. (177 mL) water

INSTRUCTIONS

1. Sauté onion and garlic in oil until soft.
2. Place remaining ingredients and sautéed mixture in the blender and blend until combined.
3. Pour into a heavy-bottomed saucepan, cover, and stir frequently over medium heat, bringing to a boil. Simmer for 5 minutes.

VARIATIONS

Use agave or maple syrup instead of honey. Experiment with the herbs to find the perfect amounts for your family's taste buds. Want a chunkier sauce? Replace 1 cup (248 g) of the tomato sauce with petite canned tomatoes. Whiz only briefly.

SERVING SUGGESTIONS

This sauce is perfect with pasta, Tofu Meatballs (p. 66), Luke's Lentils (p. 89), or anywhere else you need a seasoned tomato sauce.

PLANNING AHEAD

This sauce can be made in advance and stored for a few days in an airtight container in the refrigerator.

AMERICAN KETCHUP

"The LORD is my shepherd; I shall not want." Psalm 23:1

What are burgers, sandwiches, or french fries without ketchup? Incomplete! This ketchup provides excellent flavor without the stomach-irritating effects of the vinegar found in store-bought ketchup.

◆

INGREDIENTS

1 medium onion, diced

2 garlic cloves, minced

3 Tbsp. (45 mL) lemon juice

1 can (28 oz./794 g) tomatoes, whole or diced

1 can (12 oz./340 g) tomato paste

1 tsp. (6 g) salt

4 Tbsp. (84 g) honey

15 dates

1/4 c. (59 mL) water

2 Tbsp. (24 g) coconut sugar

Dash of cayenne (optional)

INSTRUCTIONS

1. Cook all ingredients together for 25–30 minutes.
2. Pour into a blender and blend until smooth.

VARIATIONS

Use agave or maple syrup instead of honey.

SERVING SUGGESTIONS

This is a delicious ketchup for burgers, Oven French Fries (p. 98), or Potato Patties (p. 34).

PLANNING AHEAD

This recipe may make more ketchup than needed right away. It freezes well in an airtight container for several months. You may find it helpful to freeze the ketchup in an ice cube tray. Once frozen, remove cubes from the tray and store in an airtight bag.

PLANT-BASED MAYONNAISE

"Behold, I have graven thee upon the palms of my hands..." Isaiah 49:16

This recipe holds a special place in our family, with nearly all my children memorizing it. As soon as they could read, each of my children received a blank notebook in which I wrote each recipe he or she mastered. This mayonnaise/sour cream was consistently one of the first to be added!

◆

INGREDIENTS

12.3 oz. (349 g) soft or firm silken tofu

3/4 c. (177 mL) water

3/4 c. (180 mL) avocado oil

1/2 c. (120 mL) lemon juice

1 1/2 tsp. (9 g) salt

2 tsp. (5 g) onion powder

1/2 tsp. (2 g) garlic powder

INSTRUCTIONS

1. Place all ingredients in a blender and blend until creamy.

VARIATIONS

Rice Mayo: Instead of tofu, add 1–1 1/2 cups (200–300 g) brown or white rice, cooked and still hot, to the blender. Decrease lemon juice to 1/3 cup (80 mL).

Cashew Mayo: Instead of tofu, add 1/2 cup (64 g) raw cashews to the blender. Decrease water to 1/2 cup (118 mL), decrease lemon juice to 1/4 cup (60 mL), decrease salt to 1/2 teaspoon (3 g), and decrease onion powder to 1 teaspoon (2.4 g). With your blender on high, drizzle 1/4–1/3 cup (60–80 mL) avocado oil to thicken the mayonnaise. Once the mayo reaches the desired consistency, turn off the blender. You can also experiment with blanched almonds for a whiter mayo or opt for Brazil nuts for a richer, creamier texture.

SERVING SUGGESTIONS

This mayo works well for any of my recipes that call for mayo. Add taco seasoning and use it as the dressing for Taco Salad (p. 126). The rice version of this mayo will set up nicely into a firmer dip like sour cream.

PLANNING AHEAD

This mayo will keep for up to one week in an airtight container in the refrigerator. It can be served hot or cold.

Sweet Extras

CRANBERRY RELISH

"Your Father knoweth what things ye have need of, before ye ask him." Matthew 6:8

It was the Sunday before Thanksgiving, and we were a few days away from being homeless. We were in the midst of a sudden and unexpected move from the house my husband built. An hour before we were set to move into the house we had found to rent, we were informed that it was no longer available. Amid this loss and chaos, our friends Dan and Tarra opened their home to our entire family of seven. We continued moving out and cleaning our home for the next few days, and Thanksgiving Day arrived with all seven of us still busy cleaning. Mid-morning, Tarra's dad, Grandpa Loren, called and told us that they would not eat their Thanksgiving dinner without us. Friends became family that day. It was a wonderful dinner, complete with this Cranberry Relish. It is now a treasured recipe and reminds me of the true spirit of Thanksgiving: love, friendship, and hospitality.

INGREDIENTS

2 c. (240 g) raw cranberries, washed

1 whole orange, washed, zested, and peeled

2 apples, cored

1 c. (192 g) coconut sugar

1 c. (109 g) pecans (optional)

INSTRUCTIONS

1. Add the fruit and orange zest to a food processor with the blade attachment and blend or pulse to your desired consistency.
2. Add the sugar and pecans, pulsing briefly to combine.
3. Chill and serve.

VARIATIONS

Use 1/2 cup (168 g) agave instead of coconut sugar.

SERVING SUGGESTIONS

This relish is a great addition to a holiday meal. Pair it with mashed potatoes, Sue's Homestyle Gravy (p. 161), steamed broccoli or cooked frozen peas, Holiday Tofu Roast (p.78), and Aunt Greta's Green Salad (p. 109) for a meal "fit for a king"! Have leftover relish after the party? Use it on crackers or your favorite bread!

PLANNING AHEAD

This relish maintains its freshness in the refrigerator for several days when stored in an airtight container.

GRANDMA EUNICE'S BLUEBERRY SAUCE

"For I am not ashamed of the gospel of Christ: for it is the power of God unto salvation to every one that believeth..." Romans 1:16

What do your children need when their grandmas live 700 and 1,000 miles away? An honorary grandma! Someone who cares, brings meals for new parents, attends birthday parties, babysits, and even comes to music recitals to hear "Twinkle, Twinkle, Little Star." Our family has been blessed with an adopted grandma known as Grandma Eunice. She has a passion for blueberries, buying a semi-truckload each summer the past several decades. While she sells most of them, she keeps enough to always have some for blueberry crisp or sauce on pancakes. Her love for blueberries has rubbed off on us over the years!

INGREDIENTS

2 c. (376 g) blueberries, fresh or frozen

2 c. (473 mL) water, divided

1/2 c. (170 g) honey

4 Tbsp. (32 g) cornstarch

INSTRUCTIONS

1. In a 3-quart (3 L) heavy-bottomed saucepan, bring the blueberries and 1 cup (237 mL) water to a boil.
2. Add the honey and reduce the heat to keep it simmering.
3. In a cup, mix the cornstarch with the remaining 1 cup (237 mL) water.
4. Pour this mixture into the fruit, stirring constantly.
5. Bring sauce to a boil and continue stirring as it boils for an additional 2 minutes.
6. Remove from heat.

VARIATIONS

Replace the honey with agave and swap half of the blueberries with raspberries or blackberries.

SERVING SUGGESTIONS

This blueberry sauce is delicious on French Toast (p.26), drizzled over a lemon-flavored Celebration Cake (p. 243), as a spread on Toasty Oat Crackers (p. 49), and with a host of other tasty possibilities.

PLANNING AHEAD

This sauce stores well in an airtight container for several days, so you can prepare it in advance if needed. However, freshly made is always the best.

PINEAPPLE DATE JAM

"I am the vine, ye are the branches: he that abideth in me, and I in him, the same bringeth forth much fruit: for without me ye can do nothing." John 15:5

This delightful jam captures the unique essence of cardamom, elevating and complementing the other flavors for a delicious and flavorful topping!

◆

INGREDIENTS

1 1/4 c. (319 g) dates, chopped

1 can (20 oz./567 g) crushed pineapple

1 can (12 oz./355 mL) orange juice concentrate

1/4 tsp. (0.5 g) ground cardamom

4 Tbsp. (32 g) cornstarch

1/2 c. (188 mL) water

INSTRUCTIONS

1. Cook all ingredients together, excluding the cornstarch and water, for 10-15 minutes on a low simmer to blend the flavors.
2. Mix the water and cornstarch in a cup.
3. Add this mixture to the jam, stirring constantly.
4. Bring to a boil and continue cooking and stirring for another 2 minutes.
5. Remove from heat and blend in a food processor to achieve the desired consistency.

VARIATIONS

Replace some of the dates with dried apricots.

SERVING SUGGESTIONS

This jam is delicious on Toasty Oat Crackers (p. 49), Sunflower Crackers (p. 50), High-Protein Waffles (p. 29), or French Toast (p. 26).

PLANNING AHEAD

This jam stores well in the refrigerator for up to one week.

RASPBERRY JAM

"Now unto him that is able to keep you from falling, and to present you faultless before the presence of his glory with exceeding joy..." Jude 1:24

Raspberries are my favorite berries. When I was a child, my mom grew rows of raspberry plants in her garden. We spent countless hours under the hot August sun picking those red jewels. We enjoyed them fresh, froze them, and canned them. Moving away made me realize how precious they were—supermarket prices spoke volumes about their value. It's my dream to have raspberry plants in my own garden one day, and I won't mind the time or sweat it takes to harvest them!

INGREDIENTS

1 can (12 oz./355 mL) frozen mixed berry juice concentrate

12 oz. (250 g) raspberries, fresh or frozen

1/2 c. (168 g) honey

1/2 c. (118 mL) water

4 Tbsp. (32 g) cornstarch

INSTRUCTIONS

1. In a 3-quart (3 L) heavy-bottomed saucepan, bring the concentrate and raspberries to a boil.
2. Add the honey and reduce heat to maintain a gentle boil.
3. In a cup, mix water and cornstarch.
4. Pour the cornstarch mixture over the sweetened fruit, stirring constantly.
5. Bring to a boil and continue stirring as it boils for an additional 2 minutes.
6. Remove from heat.

VARIATIONS

You can substitute white grape juice concentrate for the mixed berry concentrate, but keep in mind that the jam will not have the same rich berry taste or color.

SERVING SUGGESTIONS

Use as a topping on your High-Protein Waffles (p. 29) with almond butter. Spread it on Courtney's Crackers (p. 53) or Sunflower Crackers (p. 50). You'll find plenty of ways to enjoy this jam!

PLANNING AHEAD

This jam stores well in an airtight container in the refrigerator for several days.

KATHY'S CARAMEL DIP

"The LORD is my light and my salvation; whom shall I fear? The LORD is the strength of my life; of whom shall I be afraid?" Psalm 27:1

Receiving compliments like "This tastes better than the dairy version" from multiple people at a party or potluck is truly rewarding. Now you can be a caramel "queen" or "king," too!

INGREDIENTS

1/2 c. (160 g) maple syrup

2 Tbsp. (24 g) coconut sugar

1/3 c. (80 g) unrefined coconut oil, softened

1/4 c. (64 g) creamy cashew butter

1/4–3/4 tsp. (1.5–4.5 g) salt, to taste

INSTRUCTIONS

1. Place the ingredients in a food processor with the blade attachment and blend until creamy.
2. Transfer to a serving bowl.

VARIATIONS

Do not substitute almond butter for cashew butter; cashew butter is the only butter to use with this recipe.

SERVING SUGGESTIONS

Cut and core your favorite firm apples, then slice. Leaving the peels on adds color to your serving tray. Place a bowl of dip in the center and serve your festive caramel apple dip!

PLANNING AHEAD

This dip can be prepared a few minutes to a few days ahead of your desired serving time. Keep in mind that, when chilled, the consistency will become firmer and will soften as it warms up.

BUTTERSCOTCH SAUCE

"The LORD is nigh unto all them that call upon him, to all that call upon him in truth." Psalm 145:18

This butterscotch sauce is fantastic! I love butterscotch-flavored treats, and, as you may know, finding plant-based options can be challenging and expensive.

This sauce provides a tasty and inexpensive option your whole family will love!

◆

INGREDIENTS

1/2 c. (96 g) coconut sugar

6 Tbsp. (89 g) maple syrup

2 Tbsp. (28 g) Butterless Butter (p. 150)

1 tsp. (5 mL) vanilla

1/4 tsp. (1.5 g) salt

1/4 c. (60 g) full-fat coconut milk

INSTRUCTIONS

1. Combine sugar and syrup and heat on low until sugar melts. Increase heat to bring to a boil.
2. Reduce heat to keep it simmering for 5 minutes. Do not stir.
3. Remove from heat. Add butter, vanilla, and salt, but do not stir. Allow sauce to sit for 5 minutes.
4. Beat in coconut milk until creamy.
5. Store in refrigerator.

VARIATIONS

Use maple sugar or palm sugar instead of coconut sugar.

SERVING SUGGESTIONS

Drizzle this over whipped cream on top of Perfect Pumpkin Pie (p. 221), use as a garnish on Tapioca Pudding (p. 237), or serve over a slice of Celebration Cake (p. 243).

PLANNING AHEAD

This sauce can be kept on hand in the refrigerator and lasts for several weeks.

COCONUT WHIPPED CREAM

"God is our refuge and strength, a very present help in trouble." Psalm 46:1

I love making this whipped cream! For the wedding of one of my sons, I frosted the entire cake with this snow-white whipped cream and adorned it with fresh raspberries, strawberries, and blueberries. It was one of the most beautiful cakes I have ever made. For best results, choose a coconut milk brand with minimal water content. If you're new to working with coconut milk, try several brands, refrigerate them, and experiment until you find one that works for you. Don't get discouraged if your first attempt doesn't meet your expectations—keep trying until you find a brand that has 14 grams of fat per serving.

◆

INGREDIENTS

13.5 oz. (398 g) coconut milk, chilled for at least 48 hours at the back of your refrigerator. *(The coconut milk must have at least 14 grams of fat per 1/3-c./120 g serving.)*

1/2 c. (86 g) maple sugar

1/2 tsp. (2.5 mL) vanilla

1/8 tsp. (0.8 g) salt

INSTRUCTIONS

1. Place the mixing bowl and wire whip attachment from your stand mixer in the freezer for 15 minutes. Chilling is crucial.
2. Turn the can of coconut milk upside down before opening. Open and drain off the water. Save the water for other uses.
3. Whip the coconut milk at the highest speed for 3–4 minutes.
4. Add the remaining ingredients.
5. Continue whipping for an additional 1–2 minutes, until the cream is light, fluffy, and doesn't run. If desired consistency is not achieved, chill the whipper, bowl, and cream in the freezer for 10–20 minutes before resuming whipping.

VARIATIONS

Use 1/3 cup (112 g) honey, agave, maple syrup, or coconut sugar for different colors and flavors. For the whitest possible cream, use organic powdered sugar. Note that the choice of liquid sweeteners can impact the whipped cream's consistency. Experiment with different coconut milk brands to find one with the least water content for optimal results.

SERVING SUGGESTIONS

This is the perfect topping for Perfect Pumpkin Pie (p. 221), Peach Pie (p. 225), Blueberry-Peach Crisp (p. 230), Creamy Fruit and Rice Salad (p. 25), and more.

PLANNING AHEAD

Refrigerate for up to one week; it won't separate. You can also freeze it in an airtight container and thaw in the refrigerator when needed.

TOFU WHIPPED CREAM

"And it shall be said in that day, Lo, this is our God; we have waited for him, and he will save us: this is the LORD; we have waited for him, we will be glad and rejoice in his salvation." Isaiah 25:9

This whipped cream turns out perfect every time, even if it's your first time! This is one of the first recipes I taught each of my children to make.

◆

INGREDIENTS

12.3 oz. (349 g) soft or firm silken tofu

1/3 c. (80 mL) avocado oil

1/3 c. (79 mL) water

4 Tbsp. (48 g) coconut sugar

1 Tbsp. (15 mL) lemon juice

1/8 tsp. (0.8 g) salt

INSTRUCTIONS

1. Place all ingredients in a blender and blend until smooth.
2. Refrigerate for up to 5 days.

VARIATIONS

Experiment with different sweeteners to find the one that results in the color and consistency you prefer. If using a liquid sweetener, such as honey or maple syrup, reduce the water by the same amount as the sweetener to maintain the desired consistency.

SERVING SUGGESTIONS

This cream is quick to make, has a heavier texture than my Coconut Whipped Cream (p. 190), and is a delicious choice for Creamy Fruit and Rice Salad (p. 25) or your favorite pie.

PLANNING AHEAD

This cream will stay fresh in the fridge for up to 3 days.

Desserts

OAT N' RAISIN COOKIES

"He will swallow up death in victory; and the Lord GOD will wipe away tears from off all faces; and the rebuke of his people shall he take away from off all the earth: for the LORD hath spoken it." Isaiah 25:8

My brother, Gordon, loved cookies. As a boy, he always wanted to "test" the dough before it was baked. One day while I was making cookies, he came around with his spoon for a generous helping. As he took a bite, he paused and asked if there were raw eggs in the dough. Shocked, I responded that, of course, there were. Without a word, he walked over to the garbage can and spat out the dough. Gordon never again wanted to eat raw cookie dough. I'd love for him to grab a spoonful of my plant-based cookie dough now without needing to worry about raw eggs. Sadly, that option is no longer available. It's a reminder that life is short—appreciate your loved ones today.

DRY INGREDIENTS

2/3 c. (75 g) almond flour
2/3 c. (93 g) sorghum flour
2/3 c. (85 g) cornstarch
1 tsp. (2.5 g) xanthan gum
2 tsp. (8 g) baking powder
1/2 tsp. (3 g) salt
2 c. (162 g) quick oats

WET INGREDIENTS

3/4 c. (149 g) Butterless Butter (p. 150)
1 c. (192 g) coconut sugar
1/3 c. (112 g) agave
1 Tbsp. (20 g) Ener-G Egg Replacer
(mixed with 4 Tbsp./59 mL hot water in a small jar)
1 tsp. (5 mL) vanilla

ADDITIONS

3/4 c. (60 g) shredded coconut
3/4 c. (120 g) raisins
3/4 c. (90 g) carob chips (optional)
3/4 c. (112 g) nuts, chopped (optional)

INSTRUCTIONS

1. Combine the dry ingredients in a large mixing bowl.
2. Place wet ingredients in a stand mixer with a beater attachment and thoroughly combine.
3. Turn the mixer to low and add the dry ingredients to the wet by large spoonfuls. The dough should be only slightly sticky to the touch. If the dough is too stiff, add 1–2 tablespoons (16–31 g) applesauce. Stir just to combine.
4. Add the additional ingredients and stir just to combine.
5. Drop by heaping tablespoons onto non-stick baking sheets and flatten slightly with a floured fork.
6. Bake at 350°F (177°C) for 12–15 minutes or until golden.

VARIATIONS

Substitute the raisins with dried cranberries for a tangy twist. Replace all or a portion of the shredded coconut with oatmeal to change the texture.

PLANNING AHEAD

These cookies are lovely fresh out of the oven but will store well in an airtight container in a cool place for up to one week or in the freezer for up to one month. To reheat after freezing, warm the cookies in a covered casserole dish at 300°F (149°C) for 10–15 minutes.

SUNSHINE COOKIES

"The joy of the LORD is your strength." Nehemiah 8:10

Friends are rays of sunshine in our lives. I am so thankful for the many friends God has blessed me with. There is Sally at our homeschool choir practices—always smiling, encouraging, and ready with a hug. There is Tami from church—gentle, encouraging, and always ready to ask God for wisdom. There is Paulie—quick to remind me that God's love for me is abundant, and He will make a way. As you make and bake these cookies, may their sweetness remind you of the special people in your life!

INGREDIENTS

3 c. (366 g) carrots, grated

1 1/2 c. (288 g) coconut sugar

1 1/2 c. (360 mL) avocado oil

6 c. (480 g) coconut, macaroon shred

1/2 c. (56 g) almond flour

1/2 c. (70 g) sorghum flour

1/2 c. (64 g) cornstarch

2 tsp. (5 g) xanthan gum

1 1/2 tsp. (9 g) salt

3 tsp. (13 mL) almond flavoring

INSTRUCTIONS

1. Place carrots in a measuring cup, press down, and add water to just cover the carrots.
2. Pour the carrots into the bowl of a stand mixer with a beater attachment and add the sugar and oil. Combine thoroughly.
3. Add the remaining ingredients and mix to combine.
4. Drop the dough by tablespoonfuls onto lightly greased cookie sheets. Bake at 340°F (171°C) for 25 minutes or until cookies begin to turn golden brown on the edges.
5. Remove from cookie sheets and place on a wire rack to cool.

VARIATIONS

Substitute the sorghum flour with white sweet rice flour and opt for maple or palm sugar.

PLANNING AHEAD

These cookies are best fresh. If there are any leftovers, refrigerate in an airtight container for 1–2 days. You can also freeze for up to one month. To reheat after freezing, warm the cookies in a covered casserole dish at 300°F (149°C) for 10 minutes.

OOOOPS COOKIES

"And, behold, I am with thee, and will keep thee in all places whither thou goest...
for I will not leave thee..." Genesis 28:15

Sometimes when I'm experimenting in the kitchen, unexpected and delightful creations happen that lead to the birth of new recipes! That's precisely how Ooops Cookies came to be—a delicious accident!

INGREDIENTS

1 c. (81 g) quick oats

1/3 c. (37 g) almond flour

1/3 c. (47 g) sorghum flour

1/3 c. (43 g) cornstarch

1/2 tsp. (1.3 g) xanthan gum

3/4 c. (192 g) cashew butter

1/2 c. (170 g) honey

1/2 tsp. (2.5 mL) vanilla

1/4 tsp. (1.5 g) salt

1 tsp. (4 g) baking powder

INSTRUCTIONS

1. Place the ingredients in a stand mixer with a beater attachment and combine.
2. Drop dough by tablespoonfuls onto a lightly greased cookie sheet.
3. Bake at 350°F (177°C) for 8-10 minutes or until cookies begin to turn golden brown.
4. Remove from the sheet and cool on a wire rack.

VARIATIONS

Replace 1/4 cup (85 g) honey with maple syrup and substitute cashew butter with almond butter for a more robust flavor.

PLANNING AHEAD

Store in an airtight container for up to one week or freeze for up to one month. To reheat after freezing, warm the cookies in a covered casserole dish at 300°F (149°C) for 10-15 minutes.

CAROB CHIP COOKIES

"But thou art he that took me out of the womb: thou didst make me hope when I was upon my mother's breasts." Psalm 22:9

These were my favorite cookies as a child and remain one of my top-five favorites!

WET INGREDIENTS

1/2 c. (112 g) Butterless Butter (p. 150)

1/2 c. (96 g) coconut sugar

1 tsp. (5 mL) vanilla

2 Tbsp. (42 g) honey or agave

1 1/2 tsp. (10 g) Ener-G Egg Replacer, mixed with 2 Tbsp. (30 mL) hot water

DRY INGREDIENTS

1/3 c. (37 g) almond flour

2/3 c. (93 g) sorghum flour

1/3 c. (43 g) cornstarch

1 tsp. (2.5 g) xanthan gum

1/2 tsp. (3 g) salt

ADDITIONS

2/3 c. (80 g) carob chips

1/2 c. (56 g) walnuts or pecans, chopped

INSTRUCTIONS

1. Place the first four ingredients in a stand mixer with a beater attachment and blend for 5 minutes or until light and fluffy.
2. In a small jar, shake the egg replacer and water, then add to the butter mixture.
3. Whisk the dry ingredients separately in a small bowl and mix into the wet ingredients until combined.
4. Add the nuts and chips, blending just to incorporate.
5. Drop by tablespoonfuls onto lightly greased cookie sheets and flatten slightly.
6. Bake at 350°F (177°C) for approximately 10 minutes or until golden.
7. Remove from sheets and cool on wire racks.

VARIATIONS

Replace coconut sugar with maple or palm sugar. You can also add 1/2 cup (40 g) shredded coconut and 2/3 cup (107 g) raisins instead of nuts and carob chips.

PLANNING AHEAD

These cookies are delicious, whether they're fresh out of the oven or a few days old. You can freeze them in an airtight container for up to one month. To reheat after freezing, warm the cookies in a covered casserole dish at 300°F (149°C) for 10-15 minutes.

KENT'S CAROB CAKE COOKIES

"Take my yoke upon you, and learn of me; for I am meek and lowly in heart: and ye shall find rest unto your souls." Matthew 11:29

My husband, Kent, is a talented man who has excelled as a tile installer for nearly 25 years. Although the kitchen isn't his usual domain, he enjoys making the occasional batch of salsa or cookies. This recipe is one of his favorites.

WET INGREDIENTS

1 1/2 c. (288 g) coconut sugar

1/2 c. (123 g) applesauce

1 can (13.66 oz./403 mL) full-fat coconut milk

1/2 tsp. (3 g) salt

1 Tbsp. (20 g) Ener-G Egg Replacer, mixed in a small jar with 4 Tbsp. (60 mL) hot water

1 tsp. (5 mL) vanilla

DRY INGREDIENTS

1 c. (128 g) carob powder

1 Tbsp. (12 g) baking powder

3/4 c. (84 g) almond flour

3/4 c. (105 g) sorghum flour

3/4 c. (90 g) tapioca flour

1/2 tsp. (1.3 g) xanthan gum

1 c. (120 g) carob chips (optional)

INSTRUCTIONS

1. Place wet ingredients in a stand mixer with a beater attachment and combine.
2. Mix the dry ingredients separately and then add them to the wet mixture.
3. Drop the dough by heaping tablespoons onto a lightly greased cookie sheet.
4. Bake at 350°F (177°C) for 12–15 minutes or until the bottom of the cookies appear baked when checked.
5. Remove from sheets and cool on wire racks.

VARIATIONS

Replace 1/4 cup (28 g) almond flour with hazelnut flour for extra flavor.

PLANNING AHEAD

Store these cookies in an airtight container for up to one week or freeze them for up to one month. To reheat after freezing, warm the cookies in a covered casserole dish at 300°F (149°C) for 10–15 minutes.

DATE SQUARES

"Peace I leave with you, my peace I give unto you: not as the world giveth, give I unto you. Let not your heart be troubled, neither let it be afraid." John 14:27

Both of my grandmas frequently made Date Squares or "Matrimonial Cake," as my Grandma Rogers called it. My Grandma Funk added the additional orange flavor to her squares. In my stack of treasured recipes, I have this recipe in her own handwriting. How much love and cooking each of them lavished on their families, day in and day out. How precious to think about my grandmas and what God says about them in Psalm 116:15: "Precious in the sight of the LORD is the death of his saints." Now, the baton is in my hands. How will I love and nurture my grandchildren or the children in the Bible class I teach at church?

May those memories be as sweet as these date bars.

◆

FILLING

1 1/2 c. (383 g) dates, pitted and diced

1/4 c. (59 mL) water

1 tsp. (2 g) orange rind

1/2 c. (15 mL) orange juice or orange juice concentrate

CRUMB MIXTURE

2 c. (160 g) rolled oats

1/2 c. (96 g) coconut sugar

1/3 c. (37 g) almond flour

1/3 c. (47 g) sorghum flour

1/3 c. (43 g) cornstarch

1/2 tsp. (1 g) xanthan gum

1/4 tsp. (1.5 g) salt

1/2 c. (112 g) Butterless Butter (p. 150)

INSTRUCTIONS

1. Mix filling ingredients in a small saucepan. Simmer until the dates are soft, stirring occasionally. Remove from the heat and cool.
2. Combine the ingredients for the crumb mixture. Press two-thirds into a 9 x 9-inch (23 x 23-cm) baking pan. Spread the date filling over it, then gently press the remaining crumb mixture evenly on top.
3. Bake, uncovered, at 350°F (177°C) for 30–35 minutes or until lightly browned.

VARIATIONS

Substitute 1/4 cup (64 g) dates with dried pineapple or apricots for a flavor variation that pairs well with the orange juice and rind. Alternatively, omit the orange rind and juice, replacing them with water and 1 tablespoon (15 mL) lemon juice for a brighter flavor.

PLANNING AHEAD

This is a great dessert to make ahead of time. It will store well for up to one week in an airtight container in the refrigerator.

NO-BAKE HONEY ALMOND BARS

"Because his compassions fail not. They are new every morning:
great is thy faithfulness." Lamentations 3:22–23

These bars are like my friend Carol—reliable, wonderful, and bursting with various talents and interests.
Conversations with her are always engaging, just like these bars' delightful mixture of flavors. Like Carol, these
treats bring joy and warmth to any occasion. I'm grateful for her presence in my life,
always ready to offer words of comfort and heartfelt prayers.

◆

INGREDIENTS

1 c. (256 g) **almond butter**

3/4 c. (255 g) **honey**

1 tsp. (5 mL) **vanilla**

1 1/2 c. (121 g) **quick oats**

1 c. (120 g) **carob chips**

1 c. (84 g) **toasted almonds, crushed**

1 c. (16 g or 80 g) **raisins or shredded coconut**

INSTRUCTIONS

1. In a 3-quart (3 L) saucepan, combine almond butter and honey. Cook over medium heat, stirring constantly until the mixture just comes to a boil.
2. Remove from heat and add carob chips. Stir until the chips are melted.
3. Add remaining ingredients and stir well.
4. Turn into a greased 9 x 9-inch (23 x 23-cm) pan.
5. Chill in the refrigerator for one hour and then cut into bars.

VARIATIONS

Add some of your favorite chopped fruits and nuts to make your own unique treat.

PLANNING AHEAD

These bars will store in an airtight container for up to one week. I like to make a batch or two before a family trip or to have on hand as granola bars.

CRUNCHY & CHEWY CAROB BARS

"The LORD is my strength and song, and he is become my salvation: he is my God...and I will exalt him." Exodus 15:2

Sharing these bars with friends brings joy. It doesn't take long for someone to ask, "Is there chocolate in here?" It's an instant hit every time with every crowd!

◆

BARS

3/4 c. (192 g) cashew butter

1/2 c. (170 g) honey

1/3 c. (37 g) almond flour

1/3 c. (47 g) sorghum flour

1/3 c. (43 g) cornstarch

1/2 tsp. (1.3 g) xanthan gum

1 c. (81 g) quick oats

1/2 tsp. (2.5 mL) vanilla

1/4 tsp. (1.5 g) salt

1 1/2 c. (180 g) carob chips

TOPPING

1/2 c. (128 g) cashew butter

2 Tbsp. (20 g) plant-based milk powder or tapioca starch

2 Tbsp. (16 g) cornstarch

1/4 c. (84 g) honey

1/2 tsp. (2.5 mL) vanilla

1 Tbsp. (15 mL) water, or more to thin icing to a spreadable consistency

1 1/2 c. (192 g) roasted and salted cashews, finely chopped

INSTRUCTIONS

1. Mix together all bar ingredients except the chips. Press into a lightly greased 9 x 13-inch (23 x 33-cm) pan.
2. Bake at 350°F (177°C) for about 12 minutes, just until the edges begin to turn golden.
3. Remove from the oven and immediately sprinkle with the carob chips.
4. Allow the bars to sit for a few minutes, then carefully smooth the chips evenly over the crust using a butter knife or small metal spatula. Allow the bars to cool completely.
5. Blend the topping ingredients, except the cashews, until smooth. Spread over the cooled bars and sprinkle with the chopped cashews.

VARIATIONS

Opt for almond butter instead of cashew butter and top with chopped roasted and salted almonds.

PLANNING AHEAD

You can easily prepare these bars in advance. Cut and gently wrap each piece in plastic wrap and then freeze in an airtight container for up to one month. Remove from the freezer a few hours to one day before serving and enjoy!

AUNTIE BERNICE'S COCONUT BARS

"And all things, whatsoever ye shall ask in prayer, believing, ye shall receive." Matthew 21:22

My husband, Kent, ranks this "chocolaty" coconut bar at the top of his favorite treats, alongside cheesecake!
The original recipe came from my Auntie Bernice, and I have made a few minor adjustments.
Auntie Bernice is an exceptional cook who grows a beautiful garden each year.
We treasure the moments spent with her and her family.

INGREDIENTS

1 1/2 c. (120 g) coconut, long shred

1 1/2 c. (120 g) coconut, macaroon shred

1 can (7.4 oz./210 g) sweetened condensed coconut milk

2 c. (240 g) carob chips

1 c. (256 g) almond butter

Roasted whole almonds, for garnish

INSTRUCTIONS

1. Place the coconut and condensed milk in a stand mixer with a beater attachment and combine.
2. Line a 9 x 13-inch (23 x 33-cm) baking pan with parchment paper. Spread the coconut mixture evenly in the pan. Cover with plastic wrap. Use a rolling pin to press the mixture into a dense bar.
3. Place the pan in the freezer for 3-4 hours or until the bars are completely frozen.
4. Remove bars from the freezer and cut into 1 1/2 x 3-inch (3.8 x 7.6-cm) bars.
5. Heat carob chips and almond butter in a double boiler, stirring frequently until chips are completely melted.
6. Dip each bar in the melted carob mixture and press 2–3 whole almonds on top.
7. Place on parchment paper and keep frozen until ready to serve.

VARIATIONS

Mix in 1/2 cup (80 g) finely chopped dried cranberries with the coconut and condensed milk for a pop of color. Instead of whole almonds, try topping with toasted almond slices.

PLANNING AHEAD

Prepare these delicious bars in advance, allowing time for making, dipping, and freezing. It requires a bit of a time investment, but the end result is well worth it! They will store in the freezer for a couple of weeks.

ROYAL CAROB ALMOND DELIGHT

"Surely goodness and mercy shall follow me all the days of my life:
and I will dwell in the house of the LORD for ever." Psalm 23:6

When you make this dessert, anticipate requests for seconds! It is one of my favorite desserts to take to
potluck events, and I always bring home an empty pan.

◆

CRUST

1 c. (112 g) almond flour

1 c. (140 g) sorghum flour

1 c. (128 g) cornstarch

1 tsp. (2.5 g) xanthan gum

2 tsp. (8.4 g) almond flavoring

1/2 c. (96 g) coconut sugar

1/3 c. (80 mL) refined coconut oil

1/2 c. (112 g) Butterless Butter (p. 150)

CAROB PUDDING

1/4 c. (32 g) carob powder

5 c. (1.2 L) Homemade Soy Milk (p. 23), sweetened

1 c. (128 g) cornstarch

2/3 c. (227 g) honey

1/4 c. (48 g) coconut sugar

2 tsp. (10 mL) vanilla

2 Tbsp. (28 g) Butterless Butter (p. 150)

TOPPINGS

1 recipe of Coconut Whipped Cream (p. 190)

Sliced almonds (optional)

Fresh raspberries (optional)

INSTRUCTIONS

1. Mix the crust ingredients until the mixture can be formed into small balls with your fingers without crumbling.
2. If crumbly, add 2 tablespoons (30 mL) coconut oil.
3. Press the crust into an 11 x 15-inch (28 x 38-cm) baking pan.
4. Bake, uncovered, at 350°F (177°C) for 12–15 minutes or until the edges are golden. Set aside to cool.
5. Place pudding ingredients in a blender and blend until smooth.
6. Pour into a heavy-bottomed saucepan and whisk constantly while bringing to a boil.
7. Remove from heat, stir in the butter, and cool for 10 minutes.
8. Pour the cooled pudding over the baked crust and chill thoroughly.
9. Top with Coconut Whipped Cream (p. 190) and a garnish of sliced almonds and/or fresh raspberries.

VARIATIONS

Replace sorghum flour with 1/2 cup (65 g) sweet white rice flour and 1/2 cup (70 g) sorghum flour. Spread a generous amount of almond butter on the cooled crust before pouring the pudding.

PLANNING AHEAD

Prepare the crust and pudding a few hours to one day ahead for proper chilling. Serve within a few hours of topping with whipped cream and garnishing.

JENNIFER'S CHEESECAKE

"I am the way, the truth, and the life: no man cometh unto the Father, but by me." John 14:6

This cheesecake is named in honor of a spunky, red-haired teenager, Jennifer, who could make superb plant-based meals. With boundless energy and an enthusiasm for life, she taught me this and other recipes and infused them with her contagious joy. This cheesecake has since become a cherished delight for celebrations big and small, bringing joy to family gatherings and special occasions. Jennifer, now happily married with three lovely children, continues to inspire me with her radiant zeal for motherhood and homemaking.

CRUST

1 1/2 c. (128 g) gluten-free graham cracker crumbs

1/3 c. (64 g) coconut sugar

6 Tbsp. (84 g) Butterless Butter (p. 150)

CHEESECAKE THICKENER

2 c. (473 mL) water

1/4 c. (28 g) almond flour

1/4 c. (35 g) sorghum flour

1/3 c. (64 g) coconut sugar *(maple sugar for a lighter color)*

1/2 tsp. (3 g) salt

1 Tbsp. (4 g) agar agar powder

CHEESE

1/3 c. (64 g) coconut sugar *(maple sugar for a lighter color)*

2 Tbsp. (30 mL) lemon juice

12.3 oz. (349 g) soft or firm silken tofu

2 tsp. (10 mL) vanilla

1/4 c. (60 mL) avocado oil

1-2 tsp. (4-8 mL) lemon oil or lemon extract

TOPPING OPTIONS

Raspberry Jam (p. 185)

Grandma Eunice's Blueberry Sauce (p.181)

1/2 recipe Peach Pie Filling (p.225)

Your choice of fresh fruit

CRUST INSTRUCTIONS

1. Place all ingredients in a stand mixer with a beater attachment and combine thoroughly.
2. Press into a 9 x 13-inch (23 x 33-cm) baking pan.
3. Bake at 375°F (191°C) for 7 minutes or until the edges start turning golden.
4. Cool completely before pouring the cheesecake on top.

CHEESECAKE INSTRUCTIONS

1. Boil water in a heavy-bottomed saucepan.
2. Whisk the thickener ingredients in a small bowl.
3. Add to water and cook for 1 minute, stirring constantly. Set aside.
4. In a blender, blend the cheese ingredients until smooth.
5. Add the hot mixture and blend for another 2 minutes.
6. Pour the mixture onto the baked graham cracker crust and chill until the cheese part is set (about 2 hours in the refrigerator.)
7. Garnish with your choice of fruits and sauces.

VARIATIONS

Create a delightful heart-shaped design on the cheesecake by placing a large heart-shaped cookie cutter in the center. Let it protrude by 1/2 inch (1.3 cm). Fill the heart with one type of fruit topping and the remaining portion with another. Chill thoroughly, and then remove the cookie cutter. Get creative and have fun decorating!

PLANNING AHEAD

Prepare this dessert ahead of time and add the fresh fruit garnish before serving.

1 prepared pie crust, baked and cooled

FILLING

3 Tbsp. (24 g) cornstarch

1 pinch of salt

1/3 c. (112 g) agave

1 1/2 c. (360 mL) Homemade Soy Milk (p.23)

1 tsp. (5 mL) vanilla

1 can (14 oz./405 mL) can coconut cream, chilled in the fridge for 48 hours

1/2 tsp. (2.5 mL) vanilla

1/2 c. (96 g) coconut sugar

About 4 bananas, with 2 reserved for garnish

FILLING INSTRUCTIONS

1. Whisk cornstarch and salt in a 3-quart (3 L) heavy-bottomed saucepan. Add remaining ingredients and whisk constantly over medium heat until the mixture boils.
2. Reduce heat and whisk for an additional 4 minutes.
3. Cool for 10 minutes.
4. Pour into a glass bowl and cover with plastic wrap, making sure the wrap touches the surface of the filling to prevent a film.
5. Refrigerate for 2 hours.

TOPPING INSTRUCTIONS

1. Scoop out the more solid coconut cream (reserve the coconut water for smoothies and such) and place in a freezer-chilled stand mixer bowl with a freezer-chilled wire whip attachment. Whip the cream on high for 2 minutes.
2. Add vanilla and sugar and beat for an extra 2 minutes.
3. Mix half of the whipped cream with the chilled pudding; set aside.
4. Line the crust with banana slices.
5. Pour the pudding/cream mixture into the prepared pie crust.
6. Spread the remaining whipped cream evenly on top.
7. Slice 1–2 bananas and arrange evenly over the top.
8. Chill well before serving.

VARIATIONS

For the whipped cream, opt for organic powdered sugar for a white cream. Garnish the pie with toasted coconut. Another delicious option is to use fresh raspberries instead of bananas. Use about 2 cups on top of the cooled crust, adding pudding and cream mixtures. Garnish with another 2 cups of berries and toasted sliced almonds.

PLANNING AHEAD

For the best flavor, make this pie several hours ahead. Slice the bananas on top just before serving.

BANANA CREAM PIE

"For this God is our God for ever and ever: he will be our guide even unto death." Psalm 48:14

This pie tastes indulgent but is surprisingly healthy! It's perfect for parties or for simply enjoying with your family on any occasion.

PERFECT PUMPKIN PIE

"For thou, Lord, art good, and ready to forgive; and plenteous in mercy unto all them that call upon thee." Psalm 86:5

Pumpkin pie embodies Thanksgiving dinner like nothing else! About half of our family members choose it as their favorite pie, and we find reasons to create and enjoy this special treat throughout the year.

◆

INGREDIENTS

1 unbaked pie shell

1/3 c. (85 g) dates, pitted

4 Tbsp. (84 g) honey

1/3 c. (64 g) coconut sugar

1 tsp. (5 mL) vanilla

3 Tbsp. (24 g) cornstarch

1 tsp. (5 mL) maple flavoring

1/2 tsp. (3 g) salt

1/2 tsp. (1.3 g) ground cinnamon

1 c. (240 mL) Homemade Soy Milk (p. 23)

1/3 c. (43 g) cashews

2 Tbsp. (40 g) light molasses

2 c. (500 g) pumpkin, cooked

INSTRUCTIONS

1. Place all ingredients except the pumpkin in a blender and blend until smooth and creamy.
2. Add the pumpkin and blend until smooth.
3. Pour into the unbaked pie shell.
4. Bake for 1 hour at 350°F (177°C).

VARIATIONS

Instead of honey, use agave or maple syrup. Opt for 1/2 teaspoon (1 g) coriander instead of cinnamon.

PLANNING AHEAD

Make this pie one day ahead, as it needs a couple of hours to set up. It can also be frozen after baking. To enjoy it hot from the oven, thaw and warm at 300°F (149°C) for 30 minutes.

PUDUMPTULOUS PECAN PIE

"Ye have not chosen me, but I have chosen you, and ordained you, that ye should go and bring forth fruit, and that your fruit should remain: that whatsoever ye shall ask of the Father in my name, he may give it you." John 15:16

One evening, my husband, Kent, joined my friend Kathy and me as we chose names for the recipes in this book. When we reached the pie section, he suggested "pudumptulous" for the pecan pie, and it stuck!

◆

INGREDIENTS

1 unbaked pie shell

1 1/2 c. (360 mL) Homemade Soy Milk (p.23)

1/3 c. (43 g) cashews

1/3 c. (85 g) dates

2 1/2 Tbsp. (20 g) cornstarch

1/4 tsp. (1.5 g) salt

1 tsp. (5 mL) vanilla

1 tsp. (5 mL) lemon juice

1/2 c. (170 g) honey

1 c. (109 g) whole pecans, for garnish

INSTRUCTIONS

1. Place all ingredients except whole pecans in a blender and blend until creamy.
2. Pour the mixture into the unbaked pie shell and garnish with pecans.
3. Bake for 1 hour at 350°F (177°C).

VARIATIONS

Replace the honey with agave or maple syrup.

PLANNING AHEAD

This pie needs several hours to cool and set up after baking, so you will want to prepare it the day before you plan to serve it. It can also be frozen after baking. To enjoy it hot from the oven, thaw and warm at 300°F (149°C) for 30 minutes.

PEACH PIE

"The grass withereth, the flower fadeth: but the word of our God shall stand for ever." Isaiah 40:8

This recipe began as a strawberry pie. I remember the first time my mother took me to a strawberry farm; it felt like stepping into heaven. The abundance of sweet, red, juicy berries was incredible! Later, we were given a recipe for fresh strawberry pie, which became a family favorite for the days after berry picking. After my marriage, we owned a fruit distribution business and were able to purchase fresh peaches from an orchard. We decided to try our strawberry pie recipe with peaches, and it was love at first bite!

INGREDIENTS

1 baked pie crust

4 c. (660 g) fresh peaches, chopped

3 Tbsp. (24 g) cornstarch

1 c. (144 g) maple sugar

2 Tbsp. (30 mL) lemon juice

1 Tbsp. (14 g) Butterless Butter (p.150)

INSTRUCTIONS

1. Blanch peaches by completely submerging them in a pot of boiling water for 30–60 seconds. Allow to cool for a few minutes, then peel and chop finely. Refrigerate 2 cups of the chopped fruit for later use.
2. In a separate saucepan over low heat, crush 2 cups (330 g) peaches with a potato masher.
3. In a bowl, combine cornstarch and sugar. Stir into the crushed peaches. Add lemon juice.
4. Bring to a boil over low to medium heat, stirring constantly, and cook until transparent (2–3 minutes). Remove from heat.
5. Stir in the butter and cool.
6. Fold the remaining 2 cups (330 g) peaches into the mixture.
7. Pour into a baked and cooled 9-inch (23 cm) pastry shell.
8. Refrigerate for 3 hours.

VARIATIONS

To try the original (and delicious) recipe, use home-grown or field-picked strawberries instead of peaches. Avoid grocery store strawberries as they are often too firm and flavorless. Garnish with whipped cream and fresh strawberries. Top it with your choice of Coconut Whipped Cream (p.190) or Tofu Whipped Cream (p.193).

PLANNING AHEAD

For best results, prepare this pie several hours in advance to allow for sufficient cooling time.

HOT WATER PASTRY

"Thou wilt shew me the path of life: in thy presence is fulness of joy; at thy right hand there are pleasures for evermore." Psalm 16:11

Much as an empty pie shell is an invitation to create something greater, my friend Jeannie has a heart for children, seeing potential in who they are and what they can become. Her teaching of Bible stories inspires children with the possibilities that can be achieved through God, and her patience and skill in music education and lessons are an inspiration. Jeannie is an incredible friend and a "sister of the heart."

INGREDIENTS

1/3 c. (64 g) vegetable shortening, firmly packed

1 Tbsp. (14 g) Butterless Butter (p. 150), packed

1/2 c. (118 mL) boiling water

1/2 c. (56 g) almond flour

1/2 c. (64 g) cornstarch

3/4 c. (105 g) sorghum flour, plus extra for dusting

1/2 tsp. (1.3 g) xanthan gum

1 Tbsp. (12 g) baking powder

1/4 tsp. (1.5 g) salt

INSTRUCTIONS

1. In a medium-sized bowl, measure shortening and butter. Add boiling water and stir until the fats are melted. Set aside.
2. In a separate bowl, mix the remaining ingredients. Combine with the wet ingredients.
3. Flour a piece of plastic wrap. Place the dough on top and work the dough into a ball.
4. Let the dough cool for 5 minutes.
5. Using a rolling pin, roll the dough out between two sheets of plastic wrap to slightly overhang a 9-inch (23 cm) round pie plate.
6. Remove the top sheet of plastic wrap and flip the rolled pastry over the pie plate. Using your fingers, gently press the pastry into the contour of the pan. Using a sharp knife, trim off any excess dough on the outer rim.
7. Bake in a 350°F (177°C) oven until the edges begin to brown.

VARIATIONS

Create a whole-wheat flavor by adding 1 tablespoon (8.8 g) teff flour.

PLANNING AHEAD

This pie crust freezes well. Make several at a time, place them in an airtight bag, and freeze for up to one month. Having a pie crust or two in the freezer is convenient for making quick pies!

PRESS-IN-A-PAN PASTRY

"For I the LORD thy God will hold thy right hand, saying unto thee,
Fear not; I will help thee." Isaiah 41:13

I love how quickly this pastry comes together! Whether you're 7 or 77, it's fun to press it into a pie plate and be ready for the filling of your choice in just a couple of minutes!

INGREDIENTS

1/2 c. (56 g) almond flour

1/2 c. (70 g) sorghum flour

1/2 c. (64 g) cornstarch

1/2 tsp. (1.3 g) xanthan gum

1/2 tsp. (3 g) salt

1/2 c. (120 mL) avocado oil

3 Tbsp. (45 mL) Homemade Soy Milk (p.23) or water

INSTRUCTIONS

1. Mix the first five ingredients together in a medium-sized bowl.
2. In a large cup, mix the oil and milk with a fork.
3. Pour the liquid into the dry ingredients and mix thoroughly with a fork.
4. Press into a 9-inch (23-cm) pie plate, ensuring even thickness throughout the crust.
5. Add your chosen filling or bake as-is.
6. For an empty crust, bake at 400°F (204°C) for 10-12 minutes until lightly browned.
7. Remove from the oven.

VARIATIONS

For a delicious nutty flavor, replace 1/4 cup (28 g) almond flour with hazelnut flour.

PLANNING AHEAD

This crust freezes well before or after baking, offering a quick pie option. Freeze in an airtight bag and use within one month for best results.

BLUEBERRY & PEACH CRISP

"For every one that asketh receiveth; and he that seeketh findeth; and to him that knocketh it shall be opened."
Luke 11:10

Our son Benjamin, studying at an evangelism school in Central America, had been away for 10 months. He had regularly kept in touch, but we still missed him and eagerly looked forward to his homecoming. A few days before his expected arrival, he requested that I make this dessert and bring it to the airport. Even after experiencing the marvelous taste of fresh tropical fruits, he still craved my Blueberry-Peach Crisp!

◆

FRUIT

4 c. (752 g) blueberries, frozen

4 c. (660 g) peaches, frozen *(partially thawed for ease of handling)*

1/2 c. (76 g) granulated tapioca

2 Tbsp. (30 mL) lemon juice

1 c. (340 g) honey or (336 g) agave

CRUMBLE

1 1/2 c. (121 g) quick oats

1/2 c. (56 g) almonds, slivered, or pecans, chopped

1/2 c. (70 g) sorghum flour

1/2 c. (112 g) Butterless Butter (p.150)

1/2 c. (96 g) coconut sugar

INSTRUCTIONS

1. In a medium-sized mixing bowl, combine the fruit.
2. Add tapioca, lemon juice, and sweetener. Stir until ingredients are thoroughly combined.
3. Arrange the mixture in a 9 x 13 in. (23 x 33 cm) baking pan.
4. Mix the crumb ingredients, ensuring the butter is well incorporated.
5. Evenly distribute the crumbs over the top and press lightly into the fruit.
6. Bake at 350°F (177°C) for 1 hour.

VARIATIONS

Include ½–1 c. (62–123 g) of raspberries with the peaches and blueberries. Increase the honey to 1¼ c. (425 g) for added sweetness.

PLANNING AHEAD

You can prepare this wonderful dessert several hours or a day in advance. You can also store it in an airtight container in the freezer for a few weeks. To reheat, place in a covered baking dish and warm at 300°F (149°C) for 15–20 minutes.

CHILDHOOD CAROB FUDGE

"I will both lay me down in peace, and sleep: for thou, LORD, only makest me dwell in safety." Psalm 4:8

Honey, carob, and coconut oil form the delicious foundation of this fudge.
I can't recall a time when my mother didn't make these—they are truly scrumptious!

◆

INGREDIENTS

1/2 c. (64 g) carob powder

1/2 c. (72 g) plant-based milk powder or (60 g) coconut flour

1/2 c. (170 g) honey

1/2 c. (56 g) walnuts, chopped

3/8 c. (90 g) unrefined coconut oil, warmed to liquid

1/2 tsp. (2.5 mL) vanilla

Pinch of salt

1 c. (80 g) shredded coconut or crushed gluten-free dry cereal

INSTRUCTIONS

1. Place all ingredients in a stand mixer with a beater attachment and combine thoroughly.
2. Pat the mixture into a 9 x 9-inch (23 x 23-cm) pan.
3. Refrigerate for 30 minutes to 1 hour to allow the fudge to harden.
4. Cut into squares and serve.

Note: A slight white glaze may appear on the top in some areas due to the cooling coconut oil.

VARIATIONS

Try adding pecans or hazelnuts. Experiment with crushed dry cereals for texture, color, and flavor variations. Crisp rice puffs are one of my favorites to use. Get creative with your mix-ins! Enhance the fudge's holiday charm by placing pieces on colored foil squares and tying them with a ribbon—ideal for a festive gift basket.

PLANNING AHEAD

Refrigerate for 20–30 minutes before serving to allow the fudge to firm up. Store in the fridge in an airtight container for up to one week.

CRUST

3/4 c. (168 g) Butterless Butter (p.150)

1/2 c. (72 g) maple sugar

1/2 c. (64 g) cornstarch

1/2 c. (70 g) sorghum flour

1/2 c. (60 g) coconut flour

1/2 tsp. (1.3 g) xanthan gum

1/4 tsp. (1.5 g) salt

CREAM CHEESE

1 1/2 c. (192 g) cashews, soaked in hot water for at least 30 minutes *(drain and rinse before using)*

1 tsp. (5 mL) lemon juice

1/8 tsp. (0.8 g) salt

4 oz. (114 g) soft or firm silken tofu

GLAZE

1 + 1/3 c. (237 + 79 mL) white grape or pineapple juice

2 Tbsp. (42 g) agave

2 Tbsp. (16 g) cornstarch

SUGGESTED FRUITS

Pineapple, sliced into rings

Black and green grapes, halved

Kiwi, peeled and sliced

Mandarin orange slices

Any of your favorite berries

PIZZA INSTRUCTIONS

1. Place all crust ingredients in a stand mixer with a beater attachment and combine. When you pick up some of the dough, you should be able to form a ball that does not crumble. If it crumbles, add a couple more tablespoons of butter; mix and test again.
2. Pat into a 9 x 13-inch (23 x 33-cm) pan and bake at 350°F (177°C) for 8-10 minutes. Set aside to cool.
3. Place the cream cheese ingredients in a blender and blend on high until smooth and creamy. Spread onto the cooled crust.
4. Garnish with your choice of fresh fruits.

GLAZE INSTRUCTIONS

1. Bring agave and 1 cup (237 mL) juice to boil in a small saucepan.
2. Mix cornstarch and 1/3 cup (79mL) juice in a cup or small bowl.
3. Stirring constantly, mix the cornstarch into the boiling juice. Continue stirring and boil for 1 minute.
4. Remove from heat and cool.
5. Drizzle over the arranged fruit before serving the pizza. Keep chilled.

VARIATIONS

For the crust, replace the coconut flour with sweet white rice flour. For soy-free cream cheese, use 1/3 cup (82 g) applesauce instead of tofu. When you think about the fruits you want to use, consider the color theme and flavor combinations you wish to have. I do not recommend using bananas or any fruits that soften or brown quickly.

PLANNING AHEAD

The crust can be made a few hours or a few days ahead of the desired serving time. Just be sure to have a variety of fruit on hand to make the pizza colorful and delicious! Once you add the cream cheese, fruit, and glaze, serve within a couple of hours for the best eating experience!

PICTURE-PERFECT FRUIT PIZZA

"The God of heaven, He will prosper us; therefore we his servants will arise and build..." Nehemiah 2:20

This is a popular dessert for get-togethers with friends and family! I love to serve it as a holiday supper with homemade crackers and almond butter.

TAPIOCA PUDDING

"Jesus said unto her, I am the resurrection, and the life: he that believeth in me, though he were dead, yet shall he live...whosoever liveth and believeth in me shall never die..." John 11:25-26

Tapioca pudding, sprinkled with coconut and paired with a cookie, was one of my dad's favorite treats. Though it's been over 34 years since I last cooked it for him, we continue the tradition of topping our pudding with coconut, adding carob chips and, occasionally, a cookie. While he rests, awaiting his resurrection and new life, we savor the sweet memories of our years together.

INGREDIENTS

1 can (13.5 oz./398 g) coconut milk, plus Homemade Soy Milk (p. 23) to equal 3 c. (710 mL) liquid

1/3 c. (64 g) coconut sugar

1/4 tsp. (1.5 g) salt

1/3 c. (96 g) minute tapioca

1 tsp. (5 mL) vanilla

1 tsp. (5 mL) maple flavoring

INSTRUCTIONS

1. In a 2-quart (2 L) heavy-bottomed saucepan, mix all of the ingredients together. Let sit for 5 minutes so the tapioca can absorb moisture.
2. Cook over medium heat, stirring constantly until it boils.
3. Continue stirring and cooking for 5 more minutes.
4. Remove from heat. The pudding will thicken as it cools.
5. Serve cool or cold.

VARIATIONS

Try different sweeteners, such as honey or palm sugar, for slightly different colors and consistencies. Enhance your treat by garnishing with a tablespoon of Raspberry Jam (p.185) and chopped pecans. Opt for coconut flavoring and coconut sugar for a coconut-infused twist. Garnish with toasted coconut.

PLANNING AHEAD

Since this pudding is best enjoyed when served cold, it can be made a few hours to one day in advance and kept refrigerated until time to serve.

PINEAPPLE ICE CREAM

"A new heart also will I give you, and a new spirit will I put within you: and I will take away the stony heart out of your flesh, and I will give you an heart of flesh." Ezekiel 36:26

Using a powerful blender is crucial to ensure the creaminess of this ice cream, creating a treat you'll absolutely love!

INGREDIENTS

1/2 c. (64 g) cashews

1/2 c. (118 mL) water

3 Tbsp. (45 mL) lemon juice

1/2 c. (170 g) honey

2 tsp. (10 mL) vanilla

1 c. (80 g) shredded coconut

1 can (20 oz./566 g) crushed pineapple

INSTRUCTIONS

1. Place all ingredients except pineapple in a blender and blend until smooth.
2. Add pineapple and blend to your preferred texture—smooth or with pineapple chunks.
3. Pour into a pan or mold and freeze.
4. Optional: After freezing, cut into chunks and blend again for extra creaminess.

VARIATIONS

Add frozen raspberries as you spoon the mixture into a mold for an extra burst of flavor and a delightful touch.

PLANNING AHEAD

Prepare this ice cream a day or two in advance and store in an airtight container in the freezer for best results.

CARAMEL POPCORN

"In God have I put my trust: I will not be afraid what man can do unto me." Psalm 56:11

This unrefined sugar version of classic caramel popcorn is a regular treat for our Independence Day celebrations. The kids love munching on it while we wait for the fireworks to begin!

◆

INGREDIENTS

1 1/2 c. (312 g) popcorn kernels

1/2 c. (170 g) honey

1/2 c. (160 g) maple syrup

1/2 c. (160 g) light molasses

1 Tbsp. (14 g) Butterless Butter (p.150)

1/2 tsp. (3 g) salt

INSTRUCTIONS

1. Pop the popcorn kernels. Remove and discard any unpopped kernels. Place the popcorn in a large bowl and set aside.
2. In a small heavy-bottomed saucepan on low heat, constantly stir the remaining ingredients until warm.
3. Drizzle the syrup over the popcorn, stirring thoroughly to evenly coat the popcorn.
4. Transfer the mixture to a large baking pan and bake at 200°F (93°C) for 1 1/2 hours, stirring every 30 minutes.

VARIATIONS

Add raw pecan pieces to the syrup for extra flavor and crunch.

PLANNING AHEAD

Prepare ahead due to baking time. This popcorn will store in an airtight container for weeks, but be warned—it disappears fast!

WET INGREDIENTS

1 c. (224 g) Butterless Butter (p. 150)

1 1/2 c. (288 g) coconut sugar

2 tsp. (8.4 mL) flavoring of your choice

2 Tbsp. (40 g) Ener-G Egg Replacer, mixed with 1/2 c. (118 mL) hot water and mixed together in a small jar

1 c. (240 mL) Homemade Soy Milk (p.23)

1 Tbsp. (15 mL) lemon juice

DRY INGREDIENTS

3/4 c. (84 g) almond flour

1 c. (140 g) sorghum flour

1 c. (128 g) cornstarch

1/2 tsp. (1.3 g) xanthan gum

1 1/2 Tbsp. (18 g) baking powder

1/2 tsp. (3 g) salt

INSTRUCTIONS

1. Preheat the oven to 375°F (191°C). Grease and flour two 9-inch (23-cm) round cake pans.
2. Combine butter, sugar, and flavoring in a stand mixer with a beater attachment and mix for 5 minutes.
3. In a separate bowl, mix the prepared egg replacer, soy milk, and lemon juice.
4. In another bowl, whisk to combine the flours, gum, baking powder, and salt.
5. Alternate adding the dry and wet ingredients to the stand mixer, starting and ending with the dry ingredients. Beat for 10 seconds after each addition, scraping down the sides of the bowl.
6. Pour the batter into the prepared cake pans. Bake for 20–25 minutes or until a toothpick inserted in the center comes out clean.
7. Cool in the pans on a wire rack for 10 minutes, then flip the pans to release the cakes.
8. Cool completely before frosting.

VARIATIONS

I use this basic recipe as a base for a wide variety of cakes. Try different sugars, such as maple or palm sugar, for different colors and flavors. Choose flavorings you and your family love to create the perfect cake for your celebration! Here are a few of my family's favorites:

· Coconut Cake: Add 1 cup (80g) shredded coconut and 1 teaspoon (5 mL) coconut or vanilla flavoring. Top with Coconut Whipped Cream (p.190) and toasted coconut ribbons.
· Zesty Lemon Cake: Use lemon flavoring and the zest of 1 lemon. Top with your choice of whipped cream, a spoonful of Raspberry Jam (p.185) or Blueberry Sauce (p.181), and garnish with a twisted lemon slice.
· Maple Walnut Cake: Use maple flavoring and fold in 3/4 cup (84 g) finely chopped walnuts with a rubber spatula. Top with your choice of whipped cream, drizzle with Butterscotch Sauce (p.189), and garnish with a few chopped walnut pieces.

PLANNING AHEAD

For the best taste, enjoy this cake within a few hours to one day of baking.

CELEBRATION CAKE

"Delight thyself also in the LORD; and he shall give thee the desires of thine heart." Psalm 37:4

In 1990, amidst the excitement of planning our wedding, the desire for a beautiful cake arose, and I decided to add cake decorating to my skill set. I baked and adorned our heart-shaped cake with peach- and cream-colored roses, swags, and more. After the wedding, I joined a grocery store chain as a cake decorator, mastering the art of making sugar and grease look appetizing. Just before our first child's arrival, I chose to reserve my decorating for family and friends, prioritizing my family in response to God's call on my life. Over time, my ingredients have evolved to healthier options and natural colorings, incorporating live flowers, berries, and more. I've had the honor of crafting wedding cakes for four of our children and numerous cakes—including over 150 birthday cakes—for family and friends!

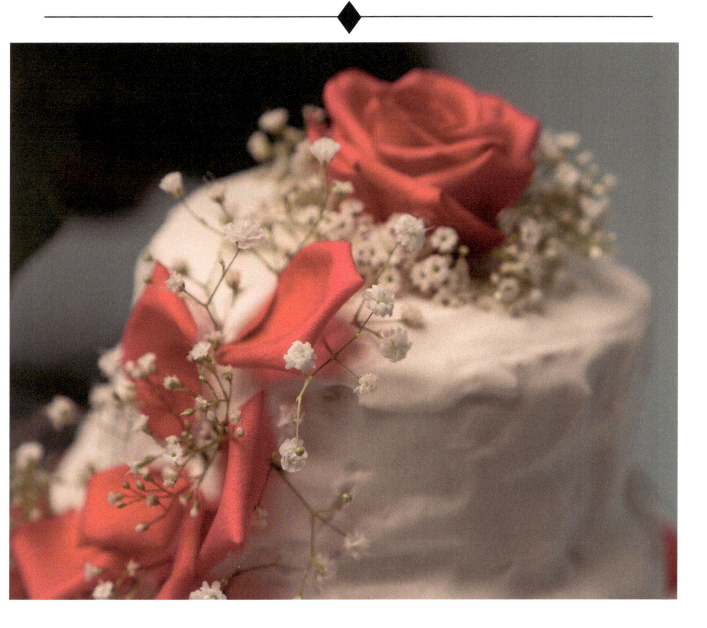

Learning More

Want to learn more about the benefits of adopting a plant-based diet? Here are seven modules I put together to give you a start on your journey to learning more. I am not a medical professional, and this information should not be used as professional advice. The online resources I recommend do not reflect my full beliefs, but they provide good information about nutrition and the food we eat. I encourage you to learn more about the food industry, nutrition, and health for yourself—it is well worth the time investment!

Part 1: Purpose to be Pure

Bible Character: Daniel

Bible Reading: Daniel 1

Thought Questions: What connection is there between verses 8, 9, and 20? Could verse 20 or the rest of the book of Daniel have been written if verse 8 had not happened?

Bringing It Home: Does God have a purpose for my life? Does He have something special for me to do? Can I do it with my current health and diet choices? As my Creator, does God have the right to give me directions about my diet? Am I ready to accept God's gift—a plant-based diet?

Inspired Insights: *Prophets and Kings,* by Ellen White (pages 479–490), offers commentary on the story of Daniel 1. Some key paragraphs: page 482, paragraph 2; page 483, paragraph 2; page 485, paragraph 2; and particularly pages 486–490.

Online Learning: I recommend "Food Choices" on YouTube. (*See disclaimer.) God has given us the power of choice. May we ask Him to help us choose wisely.

Personal Thoughts: We have all made or purchased gifts for loved ones and enjoyed the excitement and anticipation of watching them open their gifts, wondering if they would be pleased with our choices for them. As we watched smiles spread across their faces, we knew we had made the right choices! Perhaps a few days later we received a thank-you card expressing their joy over the gift. The whole experience brightened our lives! This is the way it is with God. He created plants to be precisely what we need to keep our bodies functioning at the highest possible level. He designed foods with different colors, tastes, and textures to delight our senses. He also designed the chemical compounds in plants to be what our bodies require to thrive. Components such as fiber, carbohydrates, fats, vitamins, minerals, and phytochemicals were carefully formulated to be in just the right proportions to help us thrive through each stage of life.

*This documentary does not fully represent my beliefs on every subject, but it provides excellent information regarding our diet.

Part 2: Choose Wisely

Bible Characters: Adam and Eve

Bible Reading: Genesis 3

Thought Questions: Do you think Eve realized the seriousness of the conversation she chose to have with the serpent? When, in verse 9, God asked, "Where art thou?" did He actually want Adam and Eve to express not only what they had done but also where they were in their relationship with Him? How do you feel about the mercy He showed them that day?

Bringing It Home: Do I consider it a big deal to eat food I've been asked not to eat? Does God view it the same way as I do? If God thought it was "no big deal," would He have needed to go to such extreme measures to deal with the consequences of Adam and Eve's choice? In verse 15, it was promised that Jesus would come and die to cover their sins with His blood so that the human race could be forgiven. Is eating something I know will harm my body a violation or abuse of the gift God has given me?

Inspired Insights: *Patriarchs and Prophets,* by Ellen White (pages 52–62). Some key paragraphs: page 53, paragraphs 2 and 3; page 55, paragraph 2; page 57, paragraph 3; page 60, paragraphs 1–4; and page 61, paragraphs 1–4. Praise God that He loves us so much that He created a way out of our sins.

Online Learning: I recommend "Forks Over Knives" on YouTube. (*See disclaimer.)

Personal Thoughts: Our choices today will create and determine our future. This is true for each of us academically, financially, socially, and spiritually, and also in dealing with our physical bodies. The Bible teaches us that we can choose Jesus to be our Savior. When we ask Him to forgive us, He promises us eternal life. Romans 6:23 says that the gift of God is eternal life. Can you comprehend eternity? John 3:16 also speaks of that gift as everlasting life. Why not ask Him now to be your Savior, forgive your sins, and put you on a new path? Ezekiel 36:26 says, "A new heart also will I give you, and a new spirit will I put within you: and I will take away the stony heart out of your flesh, and I will give you an heart of flesh." That sounds like a gift to me! If you ask Him, He can give you new tastes and the power to make new food choices.

*This documentary does not fully represent my beliefs on every subject, but it provides excellent information regarding our diet.

Part 3: Jesus did it for Me

Bible Character: Jesus

Bible Reading: Matthew 4:1–11

Thought Questions: Compare the conversation Eve had with the serpent in Genesis 3 and the way Jesus responded to Satan in this passage. What is the only safe way for us to deal with temptation? Why did Jesus go through this long fast? What was the purpose? What is the significance of these particular temptations?

Bringing It Home: Do I struggle with food? What and when I eat? How much I eat? How do I relate to Jesus's victory in this first temptation? Do I claim His victory by faith and ask for His strength to empower me?

Inspired Insights: *The Desire of Ages*, by Ellen White (pages 114–123). Some key paragraphs: page 116, paragraph 4; page 117; page 118, paragraph 3; page 119, paragraph 1; page 120, paragraph 2; page 121, paragraph 2; page 122, paragraphs 1–3; and page 123, paragraphs 1–4.

Online Learning: I recommend "What the Dairy Industry Doesn't Want You to Know" by Dr. Neal Barnard on YouTube. I am so thankful there are alternatives. (*See disclaimer.)

Personal Thoughts: I developed the bad habit of snacking as a child, even though my mom always prepared plenty of food for our meals. Once I was married and became the mother of a handsome little guy, I realized that if I was snacking, my son would want to as well. Deciding I needed a change, I prayerfully read the Scriptures mentioned above and the Inspired Insights, trusting in the Lord to help me conquer my habit. It is a challenge for someone who spends a great deal of time in the kitchen, but God is greater than our problems. He has given me victory in this area for many years! About a year ago, I attended a health awareness event with several speakers. One of the speakers challenged me to consider making a small and consistent change to my diet. I decided to start intermittent fasting, eating my second and last meal each day around 2 PM and then waiting until 8 AM the following day for my next meal. God has given me the strength to persevere. I know that, with a proper diet and healthy habits, I can have vibrant health for my family, allowing me to serve my God in all the ways He has planned for me for many years to come. While it is a struggle each evening to join my family around the dinner table and content myself with only the conversation, this has helped me shed the thirty pounds I gained while working at the bakery, being pregnant, nursing, and busy with life. I feel so much better not carrying all the extra weight around. By God's grace and strength, He is helping me to have victory over my appetite, one day at a time. My journey continues. I know He can help you, too!

This documentary does not fully represent my beliefs on every subject, but it provides excellent information regarding our diet.

Part 4: Which do I Choose?

Bible Characters: The Israelites

Bible Reading: Exodus 16:1-36

Thought Questions: Does providing nourishment for hundreds of thousands of people in the desert seem impossible? Is God aware of our physical needs? Does He have a plan to nourish us even in a desert?

Bringing It Home: Do I ever feel frustrated/deprived that I choose not to eat a particular food? Am I cultivating a spirit of gratitude for the abundance of foods God has provided me? Have I understood that God wants me to "eat" His Word, fresh from heaven every morning?

Inspired Insights: Exodus 15:26; Exodus 19:5-6; 1 Peter 2:9; Exodus 23:25; Leviticus 11:1-47; Leviticus 3:17; Leviticus 7:22-27; Psalm 105:37; *Patriarchs and Prophets,* by Ellen White, (pages 291-297). Some key paragraphs: page 293, paragraph 1; page 296, paragraphs 1 and 2; and page 297, paragraphs 1 and 2. *Counsels on Diet and Foods,* by Ellen White (pages 267-269). Some key paragraphs: the top half of page 268; page 269, paragraph 1.

Online Learning: I recommend "Food Inc." on YouTube. Your food-buying dollar is a vote for the industries you believe in. Use it wisely. (*See disclaimer.)

Personal Thoughts: I may have left Egypt in my body (accepted Christ as my Savior and Redeemer from the bondage of sin), but have I left Egypt in my diet? Do the ads on billboards, gas stations, TV, my phone, etc., still entice me? Have I prayed about what God wants me to eat? If I am choosing to be part of God's family, am I choosing to "shew forth the praises of him [God] who hath called you [me] out of darkness into his marvelous light" (1 Peter 2:9)? God desires that I be healthy so that I can proclaim His goodness to me and the beauty of a life lived according to His plan.

*This documentary does not fully represent my beliefs on every subject, but it provides excellent information regarding our diet.

Part 5: His Plan for Me

Bible Characters: Nadab and Abihu

Bible Readings: Exodus 24:1–11, Exodus 28:1–5, Leviticus 9:1–4, Exodus 29:1–46. In these Scriptures, we meet our Bible characters, chosen to be priests for God. It was a high and holy calling. Next, turn to: Deuteronomy 7:6–11; Deuteronomy 26:18–19; 1 Peter 2:9; and Revelation 1:5–6. In Deuteronomy, we see that all the Israelite people were chosen to show God's love. In the second two references, God calls all of His children who believe in Him to the high honor of being kings and priests for Him. Now flip back to Leviticus 10:1–11. In this Scripture, we see the God-appointed career for Nadab and Abihu prematurely ended because of their choice to drink alcohol, which led to poor decisions that led to their deaths. Finally, turn to Proverbs 20:1 and Proverbs 23:32. Here is the advice of the wisest king ever to rule, King Solomon.

Thought Questions: How could our Bible characters, who had spent time with God on Mount Sinai, be enticed to become governed by alcohol? If God dealt with alcohol in such a marked and decisive fashion, should we be ignoring the alcohol question or accepting its use?

Bringing It Home: Since God has called me to such a high position as spoken of in 1 Peter 2:9 and Revelation 1:5–6, should I use any substance that clouds my mind or that impairs the frontal cortex of my brain? Alcohol is linked to things such as domestic violence, accidents due to drunk driving, financial stress, homelessness, congenital disabilities, and marriage and family struggles. Do I want to become addicted to a substance that has caused such woe in our world?

Inspired Insights: *Patriarchs and Prophets,* by Ellen White (pages 359–362). Some key paragraphs: page 361, paragraph 3, and all of page 362.

Online Learning: "Alcohol and Your Health–What Alcohol Does To Your Body, Brain, and Health" by Huberman Lab Podcast #86. This video will help you learn from a scientific perspective what God said in just a few words. (*See disclaimer.)

Personal Thoughts: The only safe path in dealing with body-destroying and mind-altering substances is "taste not, touch not." It is time for us to rise to the high calling God has for us and turn our backs on what society and churches accept as normal. We've been called to live vibrant lives of holiness (knowing God for ourselves), to live and experience the abundance of health, and to savor happiness and joy deep in our hearts, knowing that our Creator is always there for us. "Lo, I am with you always" (Matt. 28:20).

*This documentary does not fully represent my beliefs on every subject, but it provides excellent information regarding our diet.

Part 6: Bought to Give God Glory

Biblical Festival: The Day of Atonement

Bible Readings: Leviticus 23:26-32, Ezra 8:21-23, Psalm 119:73—These verses describe how people in the Old Testament prepared their hearts and lives for their Creator God's searching. 1 Corinthians 3:16-17; 1 Corinthians 6:19-20; 1 Peter 1:18-19—These verses speak of how our bodies and minds have been redeemed by the blood of Jesus. They are not our own. They are the temples of the Holy Spirit.

Thought Questions: Imagine buying an expensive car and giving it to someone with a comprehensive owner's manual. You tell this person he or she can use the vehicle for one year while you are gone, providing the person takes care of it, and that you will want it back when you return. How would you feel if you came home to find that your car was destroyed and all that was left was a small check from a junkyard for the broken remains of your once -beautiful vehicle?

Bringing It Home: How do you feel, knowing that you have been created by a loving Creator, endowed with uniqueness and called for the high and holy purpose of bringing glory to God? Does it make you rethink your life's purpose, goals, and action plans? Life here on earth, and certainly eternal life, is worth taking seriously.

Inspired Insights: *Counsels on Diet and Foods*, by Ellen White (pages 15-40). Some key paragraphs: page 15, paragraphs 1-3; page 16, paragraph 3; page 17, paragraph 2; page 19, paragraph 3 that continues onto page 20; page 36, paragraph 4; page 40, paragraphs 3 and 4.

Online Learning: I recommend "King Corn" on YouTube. It will change how you look at the farming industry. The family farm that I grew up on has largely disappeared into the realm of nostalgia. (*See disclaimer.)

Personal Thoughts: My study of what the Day of Atonement meant to the children of Israel has impacted how I view my life, including my diet. The Israelites fasted on this day to ask God to cleanse their hearts, helping them focus on their need for Him and the serious consequences of sin. In studying Bible prophecy, I understand that we are living in the great anti-typical Day of Atonement and have been for more than 179 years. That means that the judgment of the living is going on in heaven right now. When it is complete, Jesus will return for those who have chosen by faith to claim His blood to cover their sins. This is the time in Earth's history to "afflict our souls" in preparation for this great event. We need our minds to be clear, to hear God's voice, to study His Word, and to act on the convictions that the Holy Spirit puts in our hearts. Because of the powerful impact food has on our bodies, either for health or disease, we need to each become intelligent about the gift of a plant-based diet.

*This documentary does not fully represent my beliefs on every subject, but it provides excellent information regarding our diet.

Part 7: Surrendered for Service

Biblical Principle: A perfect, living sacrifice

Bible Readings: Exodus 12:5; Exodus 29:1; Ephesians 5:2; Romans 12:1–2

Thought Questions: In the sacrificial system of worship that God instituted in Eden to point forward to the death of Jesus, the lamb was to be perfect. Why?

Bringing It Home: If all the sacrifices presented to God were to be "perfect, without blemish," how does that impact me? Because I understand and accept His sacrifice for my life, am I willing to present my body to God in the most perfect condition possible? Do I believe that accepting His gift of a plant-based diet will improve the life He has given me to be used for service? How is He calling me to serve Him today?

Inspired Insights: *Counsels on Diet and Foods,* by Ellen White. Some key paragraphs: page 20, paragraph 4; page 21, paragraphs 1 and 2; page 22, paragraph 1; page 23, paragraph 2; page 381, paragraph 2; page 390, paragraphs 1–3. *The Ministry of Healing,* by Ellen White: page 271, paragraph 1.

Online Learning: I recommend "Fat, Sick, and Nearly Dead" on YouTube. (*See disclaimer.) This documentary shows that we are what we eat. Let us consider what we eat so that we may present our bodies surrendered for service.

Personal Thoughts: The Lord has created me, redeemed and forgiven me, and promised that I will live for eternity with Him. It is my heart's desire and purpose to present to Him my best through His strength. My prayer is that this will also be your testimony. May the words of this book be a blessing to you in your journey to present your body as a living sacrifice, surrendered to the Savior for service.

21 Day Meal Plan

Want to prepare delicious and healthy meals but don't know where to start? Here is a 21-day meal plan designed to jump-start your cooking journey. Note where you can use leftovers to have meals for several days. Finish them up the next day and then proceed with the day of the meal plan you are on when you are done with your leftovers!

Week 1

Meal	Sunday	Monday	Tuesday	Wednesday	Thursday	Friday	Sabbath
Breakfast	Granola Parfaits [p. 21] with Tasty Tofu Scramble [p. 30], and Grandma Marge's Potatoes [p. 101]. Serve with sides of fruit and raw nuts.	French Toast [p. 26] topped with your choice of fruit sauce, almond butter, and maple syrup. Serve with sides of fruit and raw nuts.	Grandma's Baked Rice [p. 17] with Homemade Soy Milk [p. 23], Delicious Date Chews [p. 46]. Serve with sides of fruit and raw nuts.	Better Biscuits [p. 45] topped with Sue's Homestyle Gravy [p. 161]. Serve with sides of fruit and raw nuts.	Millet Bake [p. 14] with Homemade Soy Milk [p. 23] and Delicious Date Chews [p. 46]. Serve with sides of fruit and raw nuts.	Silas' Granola [18] with Homemade Soy Milk [23] and Delicious Date Chews [46]. Serve with sides of fruit and raw nuts.	High-Protein Waffles [p. 29] with applesauce, fruit toppings, almond butter, etc. Serve with sides of fruit and raw nuts.
Main Meal	Luke's Lentils [p. 89] with cooked carrots and Beet Salad [p. 113].	Quick Nut Roast [p. 77] with Creamy Dilly Potatoes [p. 97], cooked veggies of choice, and Shredded Cabbage Salad [p. 114].	Curtis' Oat Burgers [p. 81] with baked Irish or sweet potatoes, cooked corn, and Colorful Cucumber Salad [p. 121].	Spaghetti topped with Elizabeth's Pasta Sauce [p. 170] and Tofu Meatballs [p. 66]. Serve with Garlic Butter Bread [p. 153] and Greta's Green Salad [p. 109].	Saucy Soy Loaf [p. 70] with Grandma Marge's Potatoes [p. 101], cooked green beans, and Crunchy Carrot Salad [p. 117].	Cashew Nut Loaf [p. 69] with Stuffed Sweet Potatoes [p. 102] and Shredded Cabbage Salad [p. 114].	Taco Salad [p. 126]
Light Meal	Grandma's Cabbage Borscht [p. 133] with 3 - Bean Salad [p. 110].	Grandma's Cabbage Borscht [p. 133] with Toasted Cheese Sandwiches [p. 146] and fresh veggies.	Wonderful Wild Rice Salad [p. 129] with Courtney's Hummus [p. 165] and fresh veggies.	Grandma's Cabbage Borscht [p. 133] with Garden Tomato Spread Sandwiches [p. 145].	Garden Tomato Spread Sandwiches [p. 145] with Courtney's Hummus [p. 165] and fresh veggies.	Creamy German Potato Soup [p. 134] with Eggless Spread Sandwiches [p. 142] and Courtney's Crackers [p. 53].	Creamy Fruit & Rice Salad [p. 25] with toppings of choice served with Courtney's Crackers [p. 53].

Week 2

Meal	Sunday	Monday	Tuesday	Wednesday	Thursday	Friday	Sabbath
Breakfast	Granola Parfaits [p. 21] with Tasty Tofu Scramble [p. 30]. Serve with sides of fruit and raw nuts.	French Toast [p. 26] topped with your choice of fruit sauce, almond butter, and maple syrup. Serve with sides of fruit and raw nuts.	Grandma's Baked Rice [p. 17] with Homemade Soy Milk [p. 23], and Sunshine Muffins [p. 38]. Serve with sides of fruit and raw nuts.	Better Biscuits [p. 45] topped with Sue's Homestyle Gravy [p. 161]. Serve with sides of fruit and raw nuts.	Millet Bake [p. 14] with Homemade Soy Milk [p. 23] and Sunshine Muffins [p. 38]. Serve with sides of fruit and raw nuts.	Silas' Granola [18] with Homemade Soy Milk [23] and Sunshine Muffins [38]. Serve with sides of fruit and raw nuts.	High-Protein Waffles [p. 29] with applesauce, fruit toppings, almond butter, etc. Serve with sides of fruit and raw nuts.
Main Meal	Sunny Potato Loaf [p. 74], cooked corn, Greta's Green Salad [p. 109].	Joan's Baked Beans [p. 86] with Creamy Potato Salad [p. 125] and Kathy's Confetti Salad [p. 118].	Sunny Burgers [p. 85] with Zucchini Discs [p. 94], cooked veggies, and Crunchy Carrot Salad [p. 117].	Mac & Cheese Bake [p. 62] with Joan's Baked Beans [p. 86], cooked sweet peas, and Colorful Cucumber Salad [p. 121].	Lisette's Lentil Loaf [p. 73] with sides of Creamy Dilly Potatoes [p. 97], cooked veggies of choice, and Shredded Cabbage Salad [p. 114].	Quick Nut Roast [p. 77], with sides of baked Irish or sweet potatoes, cooked veggies, and Crunchy Carrot Salad [p. 117].	Clare's Classic Enchiladas [p. 56] with Mexican Rice [p. 58], cooked green beans, and Greta's Green Salad [p. 109].
Light Meal	Mom's Minestrone Soup [p. 137] with Eggless Spread Sandwiches [p. 142].	Mom's Minestrone Soup [p. 137] with Toasted Cheese Sandwiches [p. 146].	Wonderful Wild Rice Salad [p. 129] with Courtney's Hummus [p. 165] and fresh veggies.	Mom's Minestrone [p. 137] with Toasty Oat Crackers [p. 49] topped with almond butter.	Kathy's Confetti Salad [p. 118] with Courtney's Hummus [p. 165] and fresh veggies.	Creamy German Potato Soup [p. 134] with Get You Started Kale Salad [p. 122].	Picture-Perfect Fruit Pizza [p. 235] with Toasty Oat Crackers [p. 49] topped with almond butter.

Week 3

Meal	Sunday	Monday	Tuesday	Wednesday	Thursday	Friday	Sabbath
Breakfast	Creamy Fruit & Rice Salad [p. 25] with toppings of choice. Tasty Tofu Scramble [p. 30].	French Toast [p. 26] topped with your choice of fruit sauce, almond butter, and maple syrup. Serve with sides of fruit and raw nuts.	Grandma's Baked Rice [p. 17] with Homemade Soy Milk [p. 23], and Delicious Date Chews [p. 46]. Serve with sides of fruit and raw nuts.	Better Biscuits [p. 45] topped with Sue's Homestyle Gravy [p. 161]. Serve with sides of fruit and raw nuts.	Millet Bake [p. 14] with Homemade Soy Milk [p. 23] and Delicious Date Chews [46]. Serve with sides of fruit and raw nuts.	Silas' Granola [p. 18] with Homemade Soy Milk [p. 23] and Delicious Date Chews [p. 46]. Serve with sides of fruit and raw nuts.	High-Protein Waffles [29] with applesauce, fruit toppings, almond butter, etc. Serve with sides of fruit and raw nuts.
Main Meal	Mexican Rice [p. 58] with Get You Started Kale Salad [p. 122] and Mom's Corn Bread [p. 42].	Luke's Lentils [p. 89] with sides of Grandma Marge's Potatoes [p. 101], Glazed Beets [p. 93], and Greta's Green Salad [p. 109].	Quick Burgers [p. 82] with the bun and toppings of choice. Serve with Oven French Fries [p. 98] and Beet Salad [p. 113].	Creamy Alfredo [p. 61] with Quick Burgers [p. 82], steamed broccoli and Greta's Green Salad [p. 109].	Cashew Nut Loaf [p. 69] with baked Irish or sweet potatoes, cooked veggies, and Shredded Cabbage Salad [p. 114].	Joan's Baked Beans [p. 86] with Shredded Cabbage Salad [p. 114] and Mom's Corn Bread [p. 42].	Jonathan's Manicotti [p. 65] with Garlic Butter toast [p. 153], cooked sweet peas, and Greta's Green Salad [p. 109].
Light Meal	Mom's Navy Bean Soup [p. 138] with Creamy Potato Salad [p. 125].	Mom's Navy Bean Soup [p. 138] with Toasted Cheese Sandwiches [p. 146] and fresh veggies.	Wonderful Wild Rice Salad [p. 129] with Courtney's Hummus [p. 165] and fresh veggies.	Mom's Navy Bean Soup [p. 138] with Tuna Salad Sandwiches [p. 141].	Kathy's Confetti Salad [p. 118] with Tuna Salad Sandwiches [p. 141].	Baked Irish potatoes with steamed broccoli, Pimento Cheese Sauce [p. 157], and your choice of toppings.	Creamy Fruit & Rice Salad [p. 25] with toppings of choice served with Courtney's Crackers [p. 53].

Section Index

Recipe Index

TEACH Services, Inc.
P U B L I S H I N G

We invite you to view the complete
selection of titles we publish at:
www.TEACHServices.com

We encourage you to write us
with your thoughts about this,
or any other book we publish at:
info@TEACHServices.com

TEACH Services' titles may be purchased in
bulk quantities for educational, fund-raising,
business, or promotional use.
bulksales@TEACHServices.com

Finally, if you are interested in seeing
your own book in print, please contact us at:
publishing@TEACHServices.com

We are happy to review your manuscript at no charge.